THE PRINCIPAL AS

Instructional Leader in Literacy

Introduction to the *Leading Student Achievement* Series

The *Leading Student Achievement* series is a joint publication of the Ontario Principals' Council (OPC) and Corwin Press as part of an active commitment to support and develop excellent school leadership. One of the roles of OPC is to identify, design, develop, and deliver workshops that meet the learning needs of school leaders. Most of the handbooks in this series were originally developed as one-day workshops by their authors to share their expertise in key areas of school leadership. Following are the five handbooks in this series:

The Principal as Professional Learning Community Leader

The Principal as Data-Driven Leader

The Principal as Early Literacy Leader

The Principal as Instructional Leader in Literacy

The Principal as Mathematics Leader

Each handbook in the *Leading Student Achievement* series is grounded in action and is designed as a hands-on, practical guide to support school leaders in their roles as instructional leaders. From novice principals who are assuming the principalship to experienced principals who are committed to continuous learning, readers from all levels of experience will benefit from the accessible blend of theory and practice presented in these handbooks. The provision of practical strategies that principals can use immediately in their schools makes this series a valuable resource to all who are committed to improving student achievement.

THE PRINCIPAL AS

Instructional Leader in Literacy

LEADING STUDENT ACHIEVEMENT
SERIES

A Joint Publication

CORWIN PRESS
A SAGE Company

ONTARIO PRINCIPALS' COUNCIL
Exemplary Leadership in Public Education

For information:

Corwin Press
A SAGE Company
2455 Teller Road
Thousand Oaks, California 91320
www.corwinpress.com

SAGE Ltd.
1 Oliver's Yard
55 City Road
London EC1Y 1SP
United Kingdom

SAGE India Pvt. Ltd.
B 1/I 1 Mohan Cooperative
    Industrial Area
Mathura Road, New Delhi 110 044
India

SAGE Asia-Pacific Pte. Ltd.
33 Pekin Street #02-01
Far East Square
Singapore 048763

Printed in the United States of America.

Library of Congress Cataloging-in-Publication Data

The principal as instructional leader in literacy / Ontario Principals' Council.
  p. cm.
"A Joint Publication With Ontario Principals' Council."
Includes bibliographical references.
ISBN 978-1-4129-6308-4 (cloth)
ISBN 978-1-4129-6309-1 (pbk.)
  1. Language arts—United States—Administration. 2. Educational leadership—United States. 3. School principals—United States. I. Ontario Principals' Council.

LB1576.P738 2009
428.0071—dc22   2008035253

This book is printed on acid-free paper.

08 09 10 11 12 10 9 8 7 6 5 4 3 2 1

Acquisitions Editor:	Debra Stollenwerk
Editorial Assistant:	Allison Scott
Production Editor:	Libby Larson
Copy Editor:	Kathy Conde
Typesetter:	C&M Digitals (P) Ltd.
Proofreader:	Theresa Kay
Indexer:	Michael Ferreira
Cover Designer:	Lisa Riley

Contents

Acknowledgments

The Ontario Principals' Council gratefully acknowledges Dean Pilkington, the author of *The Principal as Instructional Leader in Literacy.*

Dean Pilkington has recently retired from the District School Board of Niagara after 33 years. During his time with the board he developed and presented many workshops on literacy, first from the perspective of a classroom teacher, then after becoming a principal, from the leadership perspective. He has presented workshops around the province on literacy, most recently for the Ontario Principals' Council, and has taught a number of additional qualifications courses in reading and computers for the Ministry of Education. For his dedication and contribution to literacy at many levels, he was awarded the Jenny Mitchell Literacy Award from the Ontario Reading Association, a branch of the International Reading Association, an organization he has actively been involved with for many years. Currently he is working on an educational reform project in Egypt with Agriteam Canada for the Canadian International Development Agency as well as instructing in language for preservice students at the Brock University Faculty of Education, Ontario.

The Ontario Principals' Council also wishes to acknowledge the contributions of the designers of the original literacy workshop: Mary Ann Alton, Sue Greer, Erin Kelly, Jacki Travers-Thomas, Wayne Gohn, and Christine Waler. As well, the efforts of Ethne Cullen and Linda Massey in coordinating this joint OPC/Corwin project are gratefully acknowledged.

Corwin Press gratefully acknowledges the contributions of the following reviewers:

Bruce Deterding
Principal
Wichita Heights High School
Wichita, Kansas

Diana Guldenstein
Literacy Coach
Stevenson Elementary School
Decatur, Illinois

The chance of any reform improving student learning is remote unless district and school leaders agree with its purpose and appreciate what is required to make it work. . . . Leadership is second only to classroom instruction among all school-related factors that contribute to what students learn at school.

—Leithwood, Louis, Anderson, and Wahlstrom (2004, p. 4)

Introduction

There is little doubt that the principal's role in a school is pivotal to all that a school represents to teachers, students, and parents (Allington & Cunningham, 2002; Booth & Rowsell, 2002; Fullan, 2003; Whittaker, 2003). An effective principal understands the dynamics of the school and facilitates the development of a successful learning community where teachers interact with each other and all of the students have an opportunity for academic and social success. The books in this series complement each other and serve as guidance to school principals, both new and experienced, to achieve this goal.

It is important to note that the principal's role is diverse, requiring skills and knowledge in many areas. The principal needs to be knowledgeable of education legislation and how it plays out in local school district policy and procedure. The principal is charged with ensuring that not only is legislation on curricula satisfied but that legislation dealing in many other areas such as inclusion, safety, family, and children's issues; criminal acts; and information meet with compliance. In short, the principal is accountable for all that transpires in the school. On a managerial level, the required tasks can surely be accomplished; however, a school is about more than rules, regulations, and compliance. It is also about people; so, effective interpersonal skills are crucial for a principal to work successfully with staff, parents, and community. Encouraging and helping everyone strive to meet their potential as contributors to learning and the school can be a daunting task. Balancing managerial and interpersonal aspects of a school while maintaining a positive, productive learning environment is challenging.

An understanding of curriculum and teaching strategies needs to be within the principal's knowledge/skill set. For literacy, a working knowledge of the language curriculum, learning/teaching strategies, and literacy developmental stages is essential. The principal must also have the skills and tools to monitor the school in order to determine if curricula are being adhered to, that effective instruction is occurring, and that student achievement is optimal. Finally, the principal must have the skills to effectively initiate change in literacy instruction where it is needed. It is to this end that this book is dedicated.

The book was written as a practical guide for principals to use as they work toward improving literacy instruction in the school and, as a result, student achievement in literacy.

Although titled *The Principal as Instructional Leader in Literacy*, the contents can be successfully used by other leaders in the school working to improve literacy instruction. Literacy lead teachers, coaches, and study groups, to name a few, will all find the suggestions a practical way to implement change. Many staff development activities, observation guides, and organizational tools are presented in the figures, ready for use at staff meetings, staff development events, and professional learning community meetings.

To begin, the definition for literacy on which the content of the book is based will be established. Because there are many varied definitions, it is important to ensure that consistency of terms is determined. As a clear definition brings meaning to the book, it is also required within a school community to maintain uniformity. One of the first tasks to be accomplished as schools move toward more effective instruction in literacy is to discuss and establish common understandings and definitions of literacy.

The historic background of the current approach to literacy instruction follows. This synopsis would be useful when working with staff to help them understand and appreciate why they may be directed to alter their current practices from those they are most familiar with and comfortable applying. In essence, they may see that what they are currently doing, although effective, can be improved on in the spirit of ongoing professional growth that leads to increased student achievement.

The foundations of literacy are explained within the commonly used balanced literacy framework. Since the model bridges a number of delivery models, staff will see that they are not being asked to completely alter the program and many of their resources and strategies will still be valid. The importance of honoring the professionalism of teachers and their ability to adapt present materials while applying a variety of teaching strategies is paramount to the success of school growth.

Another important consideration currently at the forefront of instructional improvement, differentiated instruction, is examined. Again, establishing a common understanding and methods of differentiation within a school will be valuable to future growth.

The text then leads into instructional leadership, the role of the principal. This role comes quite naturally to some principals and can be quite challenging for others. The need for excellence in instructional leadership, however, is of utmost importance to the advances made in instruction and, subsequently, student success.

Having a good understanding of balanced literacy, differentiated instruction, and instructional leadership will give you the background knowledge to help you determine how you may want to use the strategies suggested throughout the book as you work with your staff from the planning stage of a school literacy plan to implementation, employing effective strategies of shared leadership. Please note that you will want to adjust some of the terminology of the content to match your school district's vernacular and initiatives in order to make your efforts with your school community comprehensible and meaningful.

Additionally, to help you deepen your understanding of contents of the topics covered, a list of suggested reading is found in the "Must Read" section at the end of the book.

CHAPTER 1

Setting the Stage

To read is to fly: It is to soar to a point of vantage which gives a view over a wide terrain of history, human variety, ideas, shared experiences, and the fruits of many inquiries.

—A. C. Grayling, British philosopher and author

It is the goal of all school systems to ensure that students become literate, as the ability to think and communicate effectively is critical to becoming productive members of society. The school principal plays a pivotal role in this process: Effective leadership unifies a school community and helps it accomplish this goal. Having the necessary leadership skills, effective tools, and background knowledge in literacy gives the principal the credibility to work with school staff as they research, experiment, and implement successful instructional strategies. The growth in professional practices that results has a direct impact on the academic success of the students.

This book begins with the basic understanding of literacy, how instruction has changed over the years, and the role of instructional leader. The foundations established here in Chapter 1 will be supported throughout the text by effective activities and tools a principal can employ within the school community.

DEFINING LITERACY

Literacy has been defined in a multitude of ways. The United Nations Educational, Scientific, and Cultural Organization (UNESCO) expressed it this way in a statement for the United Nations Literacy Debate (2003):

> Literacy is about more than reading and writing—it is about how we communicate in society. It is about social practices, about knowledge, language, and culture. Those who use literacy take it for granted—but those who cannot use it are excluded from much communication in today's world. (UNESCO as cited in Ontario Ministry of Education, 2004)

With that in mind, for this book, literacy is considered to be the ability of an individual to read, comprehend, make connections, and respond to text and is foundational to success in a text-rich society. A literate person is able to process information and communicate effectively with others in writing, speech, and visual representation, giving, receiving, and making sense of information. The individual is able to function productively within a society where independence requires reading and writing mastery. Functioning in such an environment requires, at the most basic level, the ability to read signs, complete forms, and follow written directions. The demand for much higher levels of literacy, however, is more widely expected.

It is the challenge of school systems to prepare students to succeed and become valued, contributing members of society. Many believe it is through literacy instruction that much of this is accomplished. Through effective instruction in the areas of language development—reading, writing, listening, speaking, viewing, and visual representation—students learn to read and interact with text, understand content, formulate their own thoughts, and communicate these thoughts with others. Whatever role an individual has in society, all of these actions occur daily to some degree.

When discussing literacy with the staff you may consider reflecting on the UNESCO definition and the Grayling quote at the beginning of this chapter. Just as establishing what literacy means for the purpose of this book is necessary for you to attach meaning to the contents, establishing what literacy means to a school community will help attach meaning to a school's literacy initiative.

Since literacy affects progress in all of the other educational disciplines, successful acquisition of literacy skills is paramount. Students well equipped with literacy skills are, logically, more likely to experience success across the curriculum. As a result, there could be a decrease in student dissatisfaction and disillusionment with school and, therefore, a reduction in dropout rates and adult illiteracy. Principals and the school staffs, regardless of subject specialty, face the challenge of delivering the most effective literacy instruction to promote success for all students.

Mastery of skills in effective writing, speaking, thinking, and presentation is required to complement and complete the growth of reading ability (Cunningham, Hall, & Sigmon, 1999).

A BRIEF, RECENT HISTORY OF LITERACY INSTRUCTION

Good educators instinctively strive to improve instruction. This has led to some excellent, as well as some questionable, classroom practices. The field of education has, over the years, weathered many philosophies on instruction and learning. Some have gained more popularity; some have faded into oblivion. Others have been so modified that the original model has been lost. The need to consolidate years of research and practice and to extract understanding of effective instruction and valid strategies was identified by the Congress of the United States in 1997. The National Reading Panel (n.d.), composed of experts from many levels in the field of education, was instructed "to assess the status of research-based knowledge, including the effectiveness of various approaches to teaching children to read." It was charged with providing a report that "should present the panel's conclusions, an indication of the readiness for application to the classroom of the results of this research, and, if appropriate, a strategy for rapidly disseminating this information to facilitate effective reading instruction in the schools." Since this report was not to be new research but rather a consolidation of research since 1966, it reflected common discoveries and highlighted the most successful and enduring models. The report addressed five general areas: alphabetics, fluency, comprehension, teacher education and reading instruction, and computer technology and reading instruction.

After conducting a meta-analysis, the National Reading Panel (National Institute of Child Health and Human Development, 2000) found that phonemic awareness and systematic phonics-based instruction were critical to literacy success—components lost in some school districts implementing a whole-language approach to language instruction. The report continued by stating that phonemic awareness and phonics, although crucial, must be accompanied by fluency and automatic application of phonic skills but not at the expense of rich language experiences and appreciation. Local school district programs began to adopt models that included the identified literacy components, covered later in the book, to deliver comprehension language instruction often dubbed the balanced literacy approach. The National Reading Panel report also emphasized the paramount importance of teacher training. Government and local school districts found the report informative and it was instrumental in shaping the direction for literacy initiatives.

Simultaneously, in countries such as Great Britain, Canada, and Australia, research review, program development, and implementation of major literacy initiatives was occurring. From their work on literacy instruction, international leaders such as Dale Willows (Canada), Patricia Cunningham (United States), Marie Clay (Australia), Carmel Crevalo (Australia), and Irene Fountas and Gay Su Pinnell (Australia) have emerged to lead, inspire, and sustain the literacy movement.

Globally, many countries concerned with the importance of their students eventually competing on the global market are, based on data, striving to develop effective literacy instruction in schools. An example is the testing of twelve-year-old students in mathematics, problem solving, reading literacy, and scientific literacy conducted under the direction of The Organization for Economic Cooperation and Development (OECD) through the Program for International Student Assessment (PISA) in 43 countries in 2000, 41 countries in 2003, and 58 countries by 2006. The next reading tests are scheduled to take place in 2009. International standards in reading, mathematics, and science established by this process facilitated the comparison of students' levels of achievement. The collection and analysis of these data has been a contributing factor to the conscientious review and development of literacy instruction.

In most jurisdictions, the importance of basing literacy program decisions on sound research has been recognized, and the term *research based* has become the order of the day. Increasingly, prior to adopting any philosophy and model for instruction, a review and analysis of current research and data has been a critical step in making valid decisions that spend dwindling budgets on a most effective return basis. Educators, as literacy program developers, armed with an acute awareness of the research are able to have informed discussion and formulate possible solutions that can be validated and modified through pilot programs and action research. Whatever the approach, educational leaders, using the findings of literacy experts as well as the National Reading Panel (National Institute of Child Health and Human Development, 2000) recommendations, are working to develop comprehensive curricula and programs and effective teacher training to achieve highly literate students.

A commercial product, *The Four Blocks* (Cunningham & Hall, 1999), was a popular beginning point for many educational authorities. Although the whole-language instruction versus phonics-based instruction debate continues, *The Four Blocks* helped bring these approaches together as it identified strategies from both camps that, combined, led to student success. The model has increasingly gained popularity, often modified and generically named balanced literacy. Chapter 2 is a synopsis of balanced literacy and serves as a resource for school leaders who want a deeper understanding of the approach for themselves, the staff, and parents. The materials are presented in a format that can be used by a principal, as instructional leader, to help others understand literacy learning.

The impact of the National Reading Panel has played a major role in the development of initiatives by governments in North America. Planning and implementing literacy instruction is being driven by policies such as No Child Left Behind (2001) in the United States and Education for All (Bernard & Wade-Wolley, 2005) in Ontario. These documents clearly give direction to local school authorities to examine literacy instruction, set targets, train staff, and differentiate instruction so that literacy success is achievable by all students.

THE PRINCIPAL'S ROLE: INSTRUCTIONAL LEADER

> Effective principals are committed curriculum leaders who are dedicated to making literacy a school priority. (*Early Reading Strategy*, 2003)

A recurring theme in research and literature on literacy initiatives is the importance of the school administrator as an instructional leader. This is leadership that has direct influence on the process of instruction. Although schools can have effective literacy programs and students can succeed without principal leadership, those schools where the principal takes an active role in the literacy initiative have a better chance of improving student achievement. As expressed by Carol Rolheiser, Ontario Institute for Studies in Education, University of Toronto:

> Where schools have built teachers' knowledge, skills, and dispositions, where they have created a professional community, where programs have coherence and focus, where teachers' work is supported by appropriate resources, and where leadership exists to both lead and support the work of the school, there we find improvements in student achievement. (quoted in Booth & Rowsell, 2002, p. 15)

By virtue of involvement, the principal endorses improvement in literacy to students, teachers, and community. Deciding to accept the challenges of instructional leadership is a big one for school administrators. Some are content to be only school managers. The decision to be involved in literacy may be personal and out of a sense of professionalism, or the local school district may mandate it. Whatever the inducement, a principal should prepare for the role in order to be most effective. Preparation and a commitment to an initiative are of paramount importance and will contribute to success.

According to Elaine McEwan (2002):

> Instructional leaders must be knowledgeable about learning theory, effective instruction, and curriculum—the power within the educational force. In addition, instructional leaders must be able to communicate and represent to the students,

teachers, and parents what is of import and value in the school. They must be a symbolic force. Finally, instructional leaders must be skilled in the actual construction of a culture that specifically defines what a given school is about. The educational, symbolic, and cultural dimensions are critical to leadership in the school setting. (p. 6)

Once the challenge to be an instructional leader has been accepted, a principal needs to take an objective look at what skills, knowledge, and expertise he or she has to offer. Through personal reflection, an individual can determine personal readiness and then set about gaining the skills and knowledge they lack. Sometimes it is not until you are heavily involved in a literacy initiative that you realize what information you need.

Reflection can happen in a number of different ways and venues. Attending a conference or workshop can serve as an excellent starting point as it can offer some insight into the current developments and strategies for literacy instruction. Attending literacy in-service sessions with staff is highly productive as you receive a common message, reducing time required in follow-up decision-making discussions for information sharing while demonstrating your interest. An even more in-depth reflection can happen as an individual reads professional literature—the reader can set the pace, reread passages that inspire or challenge, and return to sections that may initially appear to have less meaning but are clarified later in the work. Even though the reader may not totally agree with all that is written, the advice and strategies of experts in the field are invaluable.

In schools where the principal is the only person in an administrative position, he or she can feel isolated. This isolation can make dialogue with other administrators on issues that impact their success as instructional leaders in literacy a greater challenge. Professional book discussion groups where leaders gather on a scheduled basis to review articles, chapters, and whole books on leadership can be very successful—especially for those who are isolated. This is the basis of a professional learning community of administrators that offers the principal an opportunity to discuss the role with others while not compromising relationships with the school staff. This strategy equips the principal with the knowledge and support to approach a literacy initiative with confidence. After returning to the school, the principal will be more prepared to be an instructional leader in the school's professional learning community.

Regardless of where or how a school principal acquires his or her understanding of literacy and leadership skills, the National Association of Elementary School Principals (2001) presents these six standards in *Leading Learning Communities: NAESP Standards for What Principals Should Know and Be Able to Do*:

1. Lead schools in a way that places students and adult learning at the center.

2. Set high expectations and standards for the academic and social development of all students and the performance of adults.

3. Demand content and instruction that ensure student achievement of agreed-on standards.

4. Create a culture of continuous learning for adults tied to student learning and other school goals.

5. Use multiple sources of data as diagnostic tools to assess, identify, and apply instructional improvement.

6. Actively engage the community to create shared responsibility for student and school success.

There are many other challenges principals may face in their quest to be effective instructional leaders in literacy including time, resistance from staff, and community skepticism. Suggested ideas, strategies, and tools to help you overcome many of these obstacles are covered in future chapters.

SUMMARY

Combining the principles of instructional leadership, the historic perspective of literacy instruction, the specific requirements of the language curriculum set in legislation, and the local school district literacy initiatives, a school principal can be prepared to utilize the ideas and tools in the following chapters to work with the many aspects of the school community toward ever-increasing student achievement.

For those not familiar with literacy instruction through the balanced approach widely used in school districts, Chapter 3 will serve as a summary of the approach. Even those with a good understanding will find useful professional development tools to use with staff members requiring this knowledge in order to deliver excellent language instruction to the students. Some of the materials can even be used to support the understanding of other approaches to literacy instruction as they reinforce the concept that language instruction requires addressing many components that work in harmony.

CHAPTER 2

Foundations of
Balanced Literacy

The longest distance in the world is between an official curriculum and what goes on in the mind of a child.

—Peter Schrag, author and former
editorial-page editor of the *Sacramento Bee*

Understanding literacy development in students and the components of literacy instruction enhances a principal's ability to participate with confidence in the growth of a literacy-focused initiative in the school. This knowledge is critical in order to be an instructional leader in decisions that will promote improved student achievement in literacy. With an understanding of literacy instruction, you become more adept at supporting teacher growth and development through performance appraisal programs and school improvement planning. This chapter offers information and suggests a number of strategies for the principal to use to become involved in literacy and will be of particular use to an administrator who has not worked in a school where literacy instruction and literacy success for the students are at the core of its culture.

The following overview of the basics should be enough to help the principal to conceptualize literacy components and instruction. The contents serve only as an introduction to the theory and practices of recent literacy instruction. Principals are encouraged to research more extensively to gain an in-depth understanding and then to reflect on how the information aligns with the school district's literacy plan and model. This information, along with previous experience in the classroom and the understanding of learning processes in general, will contribute to making an effective instructional leader.

This chapter covers a series of topics that link up through a number of activities the principal and staff can do together in the spirit of a professional learning community as they work to improve instruction and, subsequently, student success. The information could also be used independently of the activities to gain understanding of literacy instruction. The pattern of introducing a topic followed by staff development activities is employed throughout this book.

The chapter begins by looking at the stages of literacy development followed by the concept of balanced literacy and its program components. Then it presents a framework that can be used to organize the components to ensure program coverage. The material can and should be easily adapted to match school district initiatives before being used to initiate discussion, reflect on past knowledge and practices, and establish a common understanding for future planning within the professional learning community.

STARTING WITH AN UNDERSTANDING OF LITERACY INSTRUCTION

It is important to know where you are before you begin on a journey of discovery. Using an activity to determine what is already known, what is misunderstood, and what needs to be learned is a common point of entry teachers use when starting a new unit in class. It serves to reactivate prior knowledge, to review information, to pose questions, and to provide self-assessment for the students about their understanding. The result of such an exercise guides the teacher in the planning and delivery of a unit of study. There are many effective tools currently being used in classrooms. Figure 2.1 on page 18 is an example of one of those techniques adapted for use by a school staff. It can guide the staff development required to improve an understanding of literacy and instructional practices. The suggested activity asks the participants to determine whether the statements on literacy are true or false. To make the activity even more meaningful, participants will also write a comment about the implications for instructions associated with the statement.

The participants should be presented with a chart that only has the left column completed and the other two columns left blank. Then, either individually or in pairs, they can fill in the second column with a simple true or false and the third column with a thought about the implications. After completion, each statement is discussed. It is not important how many are correct; it is the understanding that results from the discussion that is the goal. The discussion could be facilitated by the principal or by a lead literacy teacher. Regardless, it is important that the principal participate in some capacity. Justification for the true or false responses is included in the completed Figure 2.1 to help the leader justify the choices with some background information.

The activity is intended to be fun but insightful. Teachers, as adult learners, are easily turned away from an initiative, especially if it is new, if they feel intimidated or uncomfortable. So, keeping it light but meaningful is key. There may even be a statement that they do not agree has been labeled true or false correctly. That is okay. A purpose of the activity is to start the dialogue and, as literacy is studied further, there will, hopefully, be many more opportunities for such discussions. This type of activity could easily be modified each year to reflect changes in policy or to begin discussion on a specific literacy focus.

STAGES OF LITERACY DEVELOPMENT

Children develop mastery of literacy in stages that have been generally accepted (see Figure 2.2). Although the terminology or precise level criteria may vary, it is understood that the growth continuum illustrates how students develop through stages that build on one another over the first few years of instruction. Some students arrive at school for kindergarten already well on their way along the continuum because of home and, perhaps, day care experiences. Regardless of what

Figure 2.1   What Do You Know About Balanced Literacy?

Statement	True or False	Implications for Instruction
Children learn to read and write in much the same way they learn to walk and talk.	False – Walking and talking are generally innate skills that develop naturally through social interaction. To read and write, however, children need to break the reading code, hear individual sounds, link letters to sounds, and learn to link letters to written words.	Systematic and direct instruction is required.
Phonemic awareness is an essential and foundational literacy skill.	True – The ability to hear and distinguish the different sounds heard in a word is critical in early reading development. Children need to learn that words are made of combinations of sounds. This ability is the best predictor of how well they will learn.	Children require direction and frequent opportunities for practice. Some will co-articulate (to hear groups of sounds as one); they need to be able to distinguish individual sounds.
Phonics is a critical component of reading instruction.	True – The knowledge of sound/symbol relationships is crucial. Children need to learn to link sounds to letters and be taught what the "squiggles" on the page mean.	Children require direct instruction and many opportunities to manipulate letters and words.
Phonics instruction is not necessary for the majority of students.	False – Phonics instruction needs to occur for all students in the early years. This instruction will continue beyond the primary years for those students experiencing difficulty.	Systematic phonics instruction needs to be integrated with phonemic awareness, fluency, and comprehension.

Statement	True or False	Implications for Instruction
A student's knowledge of vocabulary impacts reading comprehension.	True – The more a student has command of language, oral and written, the more likely the student will comprehend.	Introducing vocabulary first is important. Guided reading, another strategy, supports vocabulary development and then reading comprehension.
Reading fluency impacts reading comprehension.	True – Students need to read rapidly enough in order to comprehend.	Students require opportunities to read in a variety of settings and with a variety of genres. Participation in partner reading, read-aloud, reader's theater, and home reading are ways to develop fluency.
Frequent opportunities for silent reading support the growth of reading development.	False – Reading aloud improves fluency. There is no research to support that silent reading improves fluency. Poor readers most often avoid reading in silent reading settings.	A wide variety of materials should be used and frequent opportunities be made available for reading aloud.
Poor readers don't use strategies to help them read.	False – They do use strategies, but not necessarily the right ones for the right purposes.	You need to determine which strategies are being used by the poor reader through probing questioning. Poor readers often look at the first letter and then try to guess the word through context. Direct instruction and practice of alternative strategies is necessary.
Computer programs are valuable tools in	True –There is some evidence of promise in the areas of speech	Although computer programs are motivational, patient,

(Continued)

Figure 2.1 (Continued)

Statement	True or False	Implications for Instruction
building literacy skills.	synthesizers, hypertext, and word processing, but more research is needed.	and nonjudgmental, they must be used with caution. They do not replace instruction but offer an excellent source of activities for support, practice, and drill. Previewing for usefulness and curriculum compatibility is critical before using. Don't just trust the software company claims.
All educational practices are supported by strong research.	False – The National Reading Panel has referred to the evidence to see what has been effective. There is a need to move beyond the reading wars (e.g., whole language vs. real phonics).	We need to be cautious of bandwagons. There are many sound and tested teaching and learning strategies that are incorporated in a balanced literacy program. It is important to be aware of those methods with valid research to support their value.

age or where the process begins, if you were to analyze each individual's acquisition of literacy, the stages would be similar and very likely occurring at different rates. Also depending on the experiences and materials the student has been exposed to, you may see some later stage elements mastered at an earlier stage. For these reasons, the age range for each stage should be viewed with some caution.

Sharing this chart with teachers is a good professional development strategy. It will activate prior knowledge that many will recall last discussing during their teacher training. It can lead to a discussion on the importance of considering developmental stages in literacy programming for individual students. The refreshed knowledge of the stages will later add to the value of information about the balanced literacy diet.

Figure 2.2   Stages of Literacy Development

Stage 0	Preliteracy (0 to 4 years) "Emergent Literacy" ☐ Enjoys being read to ☐ Pretends to read familiar books ☐ Names letters of alphabet ☐ Recognizes some signs ☐ Plays with pencils and paper ☐ Has interest in printing own name ☐ Begins developing phonological awareness
Stage 1	Beginning Literacy (5 to 7 years) ☐ Develops phonemic awareness ☐ Associates letters and sounds ☐ Prints letters and numbers ☐ Recognizes high frequency words "by sight" ☐ Sounds out regularly spelled words ☐ Uses contextual and picture clues ☐ Writes using inventive spelling
Stage 2	Beginning Fluency (7 to 8 years) ☐ Consolidates "sight" words ☐ Expands letter–sound knowledge ☐ Reads simple familiar stories independently ☐ Practices using repeated and partner reading ☐ Develops reading fluency (speed & accuracy) ☐ Writes and spells with less effort
Stage 3	Literacy for Growth (9 years and up) ☐ Reads "for pleasure" ☐ Reads to gain new knowledge ☐ Expands vocabulary through reading ☐ Writes and spells more automatically ☐ Writes for communication with others ☐ Writes for personal expression of ideas

SOURCE: Compilation adapted from many sources.

Principals and teachers will also find the Stages of Literacy Development chart (Figure 2.2) to be a valuable tool when discussing a student's achievement with each other and with parents, especially around issues of placement and programming when it may be difficult to articulate just where on a literacy continuum a child is currently functioning. With this tool, teachers can identify areas of strength as well as areas requiring remediation or additional instruction.

COMPONENTS OF BALANCED LITERACY

Balanced literacy is a term that evolved from the work of the National Reading Panel (n.d.) discussed earlier. The panel was able to identify the key components of language instruction based on research of the most successful components from many language instruction models and philosophies. It concluded that all aspects of literacy instruction should systematically be taught in a program in which one or more components are not neglected or diminished in favor of others. It also stated that the proportion of instructional time required for each component varies as a student develops through the stages of literacy development but that the components are consistently present throughout the program. Fundamentally, the balanced-literacy approach combines the traditionally oppositional philosophies of the phonics-based approach, in which instruction focuses on the mechanics of reading, and the whole-language approach, in which the focus is on language experience.

The report identified thirteen components that should be present in a comprehensive literacy instruction program. The components may not be expressed in exactly the same terms across North America, but the concepts have become widely accepted. The rapid acceptance of the notion of a districtwide balanced approach occurred when teachers discovered that they were not faced with a whole new method of instruction. Teachers realized that many of the advocated best practices were already in place, perhaps under a different title, and that they were being encouraged to modify, add program components, and bring deeper understanding of instruction into the process. The report concludes with the concept that improved instruction is universally accepted as a major contributing factor to improved student achievement in literacy.

Components of a Balanced Program of Literacy Instruction

Motivation for literacy is anything that a teacher may do to help encourage children's interest in books, reading, and writing. This includes reading enthusiastically to students (geared to motivating, not just as a "time filler"), modeling and explaining the purpose and function of literacy as related to everyday life (e.g., reading signs and labels, writing one's name on things, reading magazines and newspapers, reading for pleasure and information, writing notes and letters, completing forms or applications), and book talks.

Phonemic awareness refers to situations in which students are being made aware of the individual sounds (but not the letter symbols) that are heard in language, either explicitly (e.g., teacher exaggerates and points out each sound in a word while asking children to hear a specific sound such as "mmm," rhyming games) or implicitly (e.g., repeating rhymes, songs, tongue twisters). Explicit phonemic activities are more meaningful than implicit ones, but both contribute to a balanced program. This is not instruction in letter–sound connections but rather in hearing sounds, distinguishing sounds, and understanding that words are a combination of sounds.

Sound/symbol connections involves the explicit teaching of the sounds of individual letters and their letter name. It also includes the connection of sounds that are represented by more than a single letter (e.g., digraphs, diphthongs, and blends) to the letter combinations. This component can often be found in teacher-guided word analysis and vocabulary development activities.

Letter formation includes children learning and practicing how to print letters both during and after instruction. This includes explicit instruction in how letters are formed, specific practice (e.g., tracing on paper, writing a letter repeatedly in lines, painting letters, making letters with clay or string, tracing in the air or sand), and cursive writing for older students. This does not include copying unless it is part of a specific letter-formation exercise.

Language development includes teacher-guided activities that promote the use of proper language (e.g., grammar, syntax, vocabulary) through modeling by the teacher and peers, both explicitly and implicitly. The activities include reading and discussing stories, grammar instruction, sharing information and experiences, questioning, and so on.

Sight words requires children to recognize and memorize words as a whole through explicit instruction. Little real word analysis occurs (few references to sound or symbol connections or decoding), and it is usually connected with learning "tricky," high-frequency words (e.g., *to, from, was, there, come, do*). These words may include days of the week, months, and names. These words are usually included on "word walls."

Listening/thinking skills includes activities in which students are listening in order to figure something out, integrate information, or answer an upcoming question. It is where the listening is cognitive (thinking and reasoning) and related to literacy and language.

Word/world knowledge relates to teacher-guided or teacher-supervised activities in which students are learning more about the world and how it works (e.g., discussions, videos, field trips) in a variety of subject areas. The emphasis is on knowledge, not on skills. The component is geared to help students increase vocabulary and understanding of types of words. Instruction would include rhyming (why two words rhyme), explanation of puns, antonyms, synonyms, homonyms, and so on. This does not include specific word analysis in terms of decoding and spelling.

Concepts of print refers to a preliteracy or emerging literacy stage and is usually emphasized in kindergarten and early Grade 1. It includes specific instruction and/or practice in learning about print: what a word is, how a book works (front to back, top to bottom, reading left to right). In later stages, this component refers to the structure of different types of print material.

Spelling addresses the specific teaching of how words are spelled, word analysis, or special strategies that assist in remembering how to spell. Included could be word families, inventive spelling, spelling dictation, use of a dictionary or wordbook, and so on.

Schema development is a means of organizing information to be learned and helps emphasize relationships (compare and contrast topics or concepts). This can include the use of graphic organizers such as webs, topic charts, Venn diagrams, or story maps, and includes activities in which the teacher develops or provides an explicit framework to guide children through reading, writing, and thinking. This component should occur specifically to give some cognitive support to students in order for them to, for example, better comprehend an upcoming assignment, make sense of information, or organize a writing task.

Real reading (fluency, text structures, and comprehension strategies) involves the whole context of learning about and actually doing real, authentic reading and not exercises or worksheets. This process is divided into three subcategories:

1. Explanation: Framework to help guide students through an upcoming reading assignment (e.g., purpose for reading, type of text)

2. Modeling: Teacher modeling the use of a comprehension strategy or fluency

3. Doing: Student participating in reading activity (e.g., guided reading, shared reading) to develop word recognition and fluency

Real writing (conventions, composition, and structures) involves the whole context of learning about and actually doing real, authentic writing. This process is divided into three subcategories:

1. Explanation: Specific instruction on the writing process, composition strategies, conventions, language structures (grammar), and the development of ideas

2. Modeling: Teacher modeling writing or demonstrating strategy or components within the context of real writing

3. Doing: Students actually doing the real writing by implementing what they have learned—not copying

Note

1. The thirteen components are not presented in any particular order, nor are they necessarily taught independently of one another. Often a number of components work together and support each other.

2. Oral language is of extreme importance. It is foundational to all components and is often a component of the variations of the model. It contributes to productive interaction between the teacher and the student as well as between students. Students that are given multiple opportunities to develop skills in oral language and who are encouraged to participate and engage in rich discussions can more easily transfer and apply the skills to comprehending and writing text. The omission of oral language in the activity may be pointed out by a participant and would be a great opportunity for discussion.

3. Instruction that encourages the use of higher order thinking skills is important in all components.

A Literacy Learning Activity for Principals and Teachers

This activity is designed to develop a common understanding of the thirteen components in the school staff, principal, teachers, and support staff. It offers an opportunity for discussion of the components and reflection on current programs. Even though the terms may vary, staff can begin to share a common language and share best practices of instruction of the components.

Activity

The principal distributes the titles and the descriptors of the thirteen components of a Balanced Program of Literacy Instruction on twenty-six separate cards. The number of sets of cards will be determined by how the participants will complete this first step. Staff members, in small groups or individually, are asked to match up the component titles to the descriptors. If a literacy lead teacher or coach leads this activity, the principal becomes one of the participants.

After completion, the activity leader facilitates a discussion of each component, relating it to terminology used locally (if different) and to the importance of the component to the whole.

Follow-Up

This activity should be followed up by discussion on components that are currently being addressed, a gap analysis, and planning for improvement. The principal's participation in the discussion is important, demonstrating support and concern for student success and acting as the individual who could facilitate planning time, budget allocation, and a system perspective.

THE BALANCED LITERACY DIET

Dr. Dale Willows from the Ontario Institute for Studies in Education at the University of Toronto (OISE) has coined the term *balanced literacy diet* with her analogy of literacy instruction to a healthy diet (see Figure 2.3). In this imaginative and entertaining metaphor, she relates literacy to something everyone understands—namely, the elements of a balanced diet. As a result, educators have been able to visualize how all the components of the Balanced Literacy Model interplay. The commentary that follows the chart reinforces the concept of a balanced approach to literacy instruction in the diet-related terms of the chart. It can be either given to the participants or used by the activity leader to assist in facilitating discussion. The metaphor presented to a staff by the principal or literacy lead teacher is a fun and interesting staff development activity leading to great discussion and understanding of the importance of a balanced approach to instruction. The chart could even be presented with one side blank and the challenge would be to fill in the connections before the discussion. If this approach is used, the first few would have to be completed together as a model.

Balanced Literacy and the Four Blocks

The components of balanced literacy can be sorted into a four block structure. The Four Blocks Literacy Model by Patricia Cunningham and Dorothy Hall (1999) is a popular framework used by teachers to help plan for instruction in which, on a daily basis, the four key areas of literacy development—shared/guided reading, self-selected reading, writing, and working with words—are included. The model is widely used and modified by school systems across North America. The components of balanced literacy have been added to the Four Blocks Literacy Model (see Figure 2.4) to help teachers see the relationship between the two and that using a model of some sort will help in the planning for program coverage. Additionally, relating the model to the diet metaphor, teachers can appreciate that the time for each block, the degree to which the block is emphasised, and the degree to which each component is addressed in each block will vary depending on the grade and needs of the students.

As already stated, before the principal or literacy lead teacher shares the information and the charts included in this chapter with staff, the material should be compared to local directives to see that it relates. A good activity for a school staff to do together is

Figure 2.3   The Balanced Literacy Diet

Principles of a Healthy Diet	Principles of a Balanced Literacy Diet
All food groups are essential.	All components are essential.
Foods from each group are required every day.	Appropriate literacy diet activities are required every day.
There are many different foods in every group.	Many different activities can provide each component group.
Consider stage of nutritional development.	Some components are more important at different stages.
Both type and amount of food are important.	Both skills and delivery schedule are important.
Balance is key to good nutrition and growth.	Balance is key to good growth in literacy.
Flexibility is necessary to satisfy personal preferences.	Flexibility is necessary to satisfy student personal preferences.
Many interesting foods combine several food groups.	Interesting activities combine several components.
Some groups and individuals need special diets.	Some individuals need special programming.
The dietician/cook/chef plays a central role.	Teacher knowledge, expertise, and style play a central role.

Commentary

1. *Variety is important:* Just as you don't like chicken prepared the same way all of the time, you should have a variety of approaches and activities to teach and reinforce the individual components.

2. *Component values change:* Just because calcium becomes less important after bone formation, you don't eliminate it altogether; you just reduce the amount. Similarly, just because children become able to decode, working with vocabulary development is ongoing, with perhaps less emphasis on word structure.

3. *Personal preferences play a role:* We all don't like the same food just as we all don't enjoy the same reading materials and activities. Varying them to meet personal preferences with the purpose of achieving the same expectation could be what is needed to make literacy "appetizing" for everyone.

4. *A combination of components:* A meal has a variety of food on the plate to make it appealing and delicious. Similarly, interesting activities will combine many components at once in interesting and motivating ways.

5. *Specialization:* Some individuals, such as diabetics, require special diets. So do students. Some students require more of something (e.g., instruction, time, practice) or specialized assistance or equipment.

6. *Creating appetite:* Dinner in a hospital is a balanced meal, but you seldom ask for more. Teachers should be the fine chefs who create and present learning that will make the children crave more literacy learning.

Figure 2.4   Components of a Balanced Literacy Program in the Four Blocks

Working With Words	Supported Reading
Concepts of print	Concepts of print
Phonemic awareness	Word/world knowledge
Letter recognition	Vocabulary development
Letter formation	Fluency
Sound/symbol connections	Schema development
Sight words	Text structure
Decoding	Comprehension strategies
Spelling	
Supported Writing	**Teacher Read-Aloud and Self-Selected Reading**
Forms of writing	*Read-aloud allows teacher to build*
Writing process	*and reinforce*
Writing conventions	Schema development
	Vocabulary development
Allows students to apply and practice	Comprehension strategies
Letter recognition	
Letter formation	*Self-selected reading allows*
Phonemic awareness	*students to practice and apply*
Sound/symbols connections	Concepts of print
Spelling	Decoding
Concepts of print	Fluency
Text structure	Text structure
	Comprehension strategies
	Phonemic awareness
	Sound/symbol connections
	Sight words
	Vocabulary

Oral Language
The foundation of literacy that supports instruction, thinking, interaction, and growth in all of the components

to compare Figure 2.4 to the existing model in the school. This would serve to deepen their understanding of the models and literacy instruction and to emphasis the importance of effective planning and instruction.

It is worth noting that the original Four Blocks Literacy Model was designed for use in Grades 1 through 3, but as the literacy movement grows to encompass all grades, it can be modified for grade or division to maintain the structure of balanced literacy instruction.

The charts in this chapter are intended to help principals and teachers conceptualize a literacy program. By being aware of the components and the need for daily instruction in each block, teachers can use the model to balance instruction and keep track of what has been taught and what needs to be covered in the curriculum. Although some of the terminology may be different, principals, with practice, can refer to the modified model when observing in classrooms. After seeing a particular activity, the corresponding component and blocks can be identified by the principal. If in doubt, it would be a good opportunity for professional dialogue in which the principal would have a chance to discuss and learn about literacy instruction from the teacher. Chapter 9 goes into more depth on staff observations and offers some instructions on walking about the school. It provides a tool to use within a school to promote professional discussion between the principal and the staff in the spirit of a professional learning community.

The Balanced Literacy Classroom

A common request from both teachers and principals working on balanced literacy initiatives is to have some indication of what the program should look like in action. Given criteria, teachers would be able to visualize their classrooms and put practices into place. Principals would be able to understand what they are observing. In some school districts, video is used at professional development sessions to help participants understand the physical attributes and the use of strategies. The use of video can be highly effective.

The confines of a book, however, require that this information be presented in list format. Although informative, lists can sometimes be misunderstood and misused. The following chart (Figure 2.5) is intended for learning, reflection, and growth, not staff evaluation.

Many of the criteria may already exist in the class. Some may be new, and others would have to be investigated, tried, and would take time to incorporate. Used by teachers and encouraged by principals, the criteria could serve as a valuable tool when discussing implementation and determining future professional development needs. This tool would be of great use in a professional learning community to guide and assist in professional growth.

Remember to update the list to reflect changes in programs and strategies before using. The users should be encouraged to collectively add or change criteria to make them as comprehensive as possible. They should also be encouraged to consider and discuss the criteria in depth. For example, when reflecting on whether the students are using reading strategies or not, list the strategies that are currently expected by program requirements of the school district. Then look at those that are being taught and used and those that have been overlooked for whatever reason. This will help focus the instructional decisions about the areas requiring more attention. Figure 2.5 is offered as a model and may not be as inclusive as you require.

Figure 2.5 A Balanced Literacy Classroom

The Learning Environment

o Provide a wide range of interesting, stimulating, and assistive learning materials: print, visual, tactile, and so on.
o Focus on what children can do, not on what they cannot do.
o Treat learning as a shared responsibility and encourage everyone to try.
o Encourage students to be risk takers.
o Integrate language learning across the curriculum.
o Provide many opportunities for children to demonstrate and share their literacy learning.
o Observe students carefully and provide appropriate materials for their level, interests, and needs.

The Program

o Schedule a large block of time daily for uninterrupted literacy instruction.
o Systematically address a variety of components each day.

(Continued)

Figure 2.5 (Continued)

o   Use direct instruction and student-centered learning as appropriate to content, students, and needs.

o   Make reading, writing, speaking, listening, viewing, and visual representation all part of the learning process and treat them as complementary activities in a variety of combinations.

o   Use and teach literacy skills in all content areas.

o   Read to and with children daily.

o   Use read-aloud, instructional, and self-selected reading materials that incorporate a variety of genres, authors, and themes.

o   Use shared reading strategies for instruction.

o   Use guided reading strategies to work with small groups of students with leveled materials.

o   Foster independent reading with leveled materials.

o   Teach reading strategies and refer to them during instruction.

o   Make reading activities authentic and meaningful.

o   Model writing for children in a variety of ways throughout the day.

o   Teach elements of the writing process and put them into regular practice.

o   Use shared writing with children to help them learn the writing process.

o   Share, respond to, and celebrate writing.

o   Teach and have students practice writing traits, conventions, grammar, and spelling in a variety of authentic, meaningful, and purposeful forms and contexts.

o   Hold writing and reading conferences regularly with individual students.

o   Provide opportunities for children to write individually, in groups, and as a whole class.

o   Develop listening and speaking skills through interaction directly related to reading, writing, and other learning activities.

o   Create opportunities for children to use speech for a variety of purposes in a variety of ways: independent, pairs, and groups, both formally and informally.

o   Encourage social talk.

o   Value and use drama regularly to extend learning and thinking.

o   Use questioning to provide opportunities for many levels of thinking (Bloom's taxonomy).

o   Recognize students' speech as a major route to learning.

o   Set aside time daily for children to come together and share the work they have been learning and producing.

NOTE: Some criteria are more applicable at a particular grade level or instructional level.

SUMMARY

The series of activities presented in this chapter can be used to help inform school staff and help them move forward with a literacy initiative. Hopefully, these activities will open up the lines of communication and help facilitate dialogue between teachers and the principal. The ideas in this chapter present a working knowledge of literacy instruction currently being practiced in many school districts and can help you become a more involved instructional leader and a confident participant in professional dialogue on literacy. That dialogue is one that happens formally and informally in the hall, at staff meetings, at in-servicing sessions, and with other school leaders. This chapter is also useful as professional reading for a teacher who is new to balanced literacy or to a literacy-lead teacher or coach who is charged with working with the school staff.

In the next chapter the principal's role in helping meet the literacy needs of all students will be explored. The background and understanding of literacy instruction from Chapter 2 will assist in the decisions that take place as the school works toward success for all students. Tools will be presented in Chapter 3 to focus discussion on student needs, differentiated instruction, and teams working to help students requiring assistance.

CHAPTER 3

Meeting the Needs of All Students

The important thing is not so much that every child should be taught as that every child should be given the wish to learn.

—John Lubbock, British anthropologist and essayist

M ost children progress through literacy skill levels at a predetermined rate as outlined in curriculum documents, but not all students master literacy skills at the same age. Some students progress much more quickly, while others lag behind. Whatever the rate of growth, teachers are required to meet the individual needs of each child. Schools recognize the need to put in place research-based interventions when a student has, for whatever reason, not been able to master age-appropriate skills. In some cases, this means closing the gap for children who began school without the advantage of a sound beginning in literacy at home. Early childhood teachers understand and use the tools that support these children. If the gap is closed, and it can be with proper intervention, these students will continue to develop literacy skills at the same pace as the majority of children. In other cases, some individuals have a learning disability or lack the cognitive ability to progress as expected. Whatever the situation, it is the legal responsibility of the principal to ensure that teachers are making accommodations and modifications to meet student needs.

Legislation in the United States (No Child Left Behind, 2001) and similar rulings in Ontario (Education for All; see Bernard & Wade-Woolley, 2005), as well as legislation in many other jurisdictions, have charged schools with the duty to make every child successful. As school principal, you are ultimately responsible to see that there is compliance with the education laws. This chapter will give you some tools to use as you help staff work toward literacy success for all of the students. In fact, much of what is covered in this chapter applies to teaching all children as each child is unique and deserves the same instructional considerations even though they may not have a formally identified need.

The model for determining student needs and the programming involved varies from district to district; however, whatever the model, the school principal plays a critical role. The principal needs an understanding of the developmental stages of literacy, the literacy program and strategies, and differentiated instruction in order to be a contributing member in the dialogue and decision-making process. It is likely that requests for special support or materials will also be channeled through the principal. The principal is then responsible to follow up on the decisions by communicating regularly with the teacher to ensure that the plan has been implemented and to determine the plan's level of success. This is then followed by subsequent meetings involving the principal designed to monitor progress reports and changes to the plan. In many cases, as the process unfolds, it is the principal who chairs the meeting with teachers, district specialists, and parents in a process to formally identify a student with special needs. This critical step can ensure specialized literacy programming for some students.

UNDERSTANDING STUDENT NEEDS

The better prepared the principal and teachers are for meetings used to identify a student with special needs, the more productive the meeting will be. The following tool, Figure 3.1, developed by Dr. Dale Willows, helps establish the areas where a student is experiencing difficulty. Within each of the processing areas (symbol coding, language, and spatial-numerical), the skills contributing to the type of processing have been listed. Preparing for the conference, the teacher underlines the areas of concern while considering the

Figure 3.1   Areas of Processing Contributing to Language Difficulty

Area 1 – Symbol Coding

Reading

- Letter recognition
- Word recognition
  - o Sight words
  - o Word analysis
- Reading fluency
  - o Slow and inaccurate
  - o Overreliance on context
    - ▪ Omission of words and parts of words
    - ▪ Familiar stories recited instead of read
- Reading comprehension
  - o Limited due to letter recognition
  - o Listening comprehension superior
  - o Rereading required

Writing

- Letter formation
  - o Slow at copying
  - o Poorly formed letters
  - o Upper/lowercase intermixed
  - o Reversals
  - o Printing used when others are writing
- Spelling
  - o Insensitivity to spelling patterns
  - o Words spelled best in lists, not compositions
  - o Letters reversed/letter order transposed
  - o Difficulty checking spelling by sight
- Written composition
  - o Written expression below oral
  - o Words omitted and repeated
  - o Word endings and parts omitted
  - o Spacing between words sloppy
  - o Punctuation details omitted

Memory

- Weak short-term working memory
- Weak phonological memory
- Weak long-term rote memory

Area 2 – Language Processing

Language development

- Phonological development
  - o Delayed/unclear speech
  - o Misperception of speech sounds
  - o Mispronunciation of words

(Continued)

Figure 3.1 (Continued)

- Semantic and syntactic development
  - o Late learning to talk, slow vocabulary growth
  - o Word-finding difficulties
  - o Immature syntax
  - o Impoverished language output

Reading

- Decoding/word recognition
  - o Weak grapheme/phoneme knowledge
  - o Mispronunciation of words
  - o Weak knowledge of word meanings
  - o Word retrieval problems
- Slow dysfluent reading
- Insensitivity to context clues
- Weak comprehension – both in aural language and in reading

Writing

- Spelling
  - o Words misspelled due to phonological confusion
  - o Voiced-unvoiced confusions
  - o Similar sounds confused
  - o Hard-to-hear sound omitted
  - o Vowels with similar place of articulation confused
  - o Weak analysis of sounds in longer words
  - o Memory for spelling of nonphonetic words weak
- Written comprehension
  - o Weak oral and written expression
  - o Inappropriate word usage
  - o Limited vocabulary
  - o Immature grammatical structures
  - o Confusion about abstract functions
  - o Repetitive language patterns
  - o Limited productivity
- Pervasive memory difficulties
  - o Short-term working memory (meaningful/nonmeaningful)
  - o Weak long-term rote memory
  - o Weak long-term semantic memory

Area 3 – Spatial-Numerical

- Weak processing of spatial organization
- Weak visual-spatial-motor integration
- Weak number concepts
- Weak right-left concepts
- Gross and/or fine motor difficulties
- Handwriting, spelling, and math difficulties
- May have weak social problem solving

data, sample work, and observation notes. Since the chart is quite comprehensive, the teacher considers all of the areas, not just those areas that are the most apparent weaknesses. This creates a concise, visual representation of the areas of weakness. The completed chart, with student work and assessment results, helps the teacher, the principal, and the special resource teacher define the needs of the student and focus on the type of remediation that should be put in place. Students will likely not have difficulty in just one of the areas on this chart, as learning difficulties are often multileveled; however, a pattern usually emerges. An interesting profile that can emerge is the student who has excellent symbol-coding skills (decoding) yet has very poor language processing skills. These are students who often "fool" the teacher initially because they appear to be able to read well, and until comprehension is assessed, no difficulty is apparent. This particular profile would indicate that more time should be spent in the Area 2 skills, with less of a focus on Area 1 skills that are already strong.

Principals who are using this organizer with teachers are finding that more time is spent at meetings on discussion of strategies to help the student and much less time on reviewing all of the information about the child in order to determine the need because the teacher comes to the meeting with a clear sense of the problem. Teachers find that using the chart helps them focus on the many aspects of processing.

After a need has been defined, a plan is then put in place. The team approach, commonly used to develop this plan, is discussed in Chapter 8. The plan will focus on areas for improvement and strategies that will include ways to differentiate literacy instruction for the student. It will also take into consideration the learning style of the student, which can be used to design instruction and materials that can ensure success. If the principal and the teachers have a good understanding of learning styles, differentiated instruction, and the curriculum, the planning time will be used efficiently and implementation can be more complete and effective.

Parent Involvement

Throughout this process, parents must be made aware of student learning difficulties, be involved with decisions to help the child, and receive progress reports. In most cases, the initial meeting with parents about literacy difficulties is with the classroom teacher and issues are resolved, but sometimes the need for more intensive intervention becomes apparent. Depending on the school system procedure, the case may result in a number of meetings over which the principal presides. It is also the principal's duty to ensure that the teacher is adhering to the program and that progress is being monitored.

These meetings may be the first and only opportunities for the principal to interact with the parents of a particular child. Throughout the process, building a trusting relationship with the parents is important. Parents who feel that the principal has their child's best interest at heart can be more receptive to some difficult programming and placement decisions.

Learning Styles

The discussion of differentiated instruction needs to begin with an understanding of learning styles. Learning styles are defined as personal qualities that influence students' abilities to acquire information, interact, and participate in learning experiences. A learning style is a person's typical mode of thinking, remembering, and problem solving. As a result, knowing how a student processes information could be the key to knowing how to differentiate instruction. For example, after a lesson on haiku poetry a student is experiencing difficulty using the style to compose a haiku poem. The teacher, rather than reteaching the concept to the child in the same style, which was perhaps primarily visual in nature, could adjust the instruction to a more tactile style. For that particular student, whose strength is in tactile learning, the ability to complete the task may be increased. That is not to say that all lessons need to match each style, as students should be encouraged to think, learn, and demonstrate mastery in a variety of ways. The point is that to avoid frustration and meet with success leading to improved attitude and future success, there are times when adapting to a learning style for the student is the best approach.

Learning style researchers have developed many models that range from a few classifications to many and focus on other perspectives such as personality, social interaction, and multiple intelligences. Some of the more well known of the over eighty models for use are the result of research and development by Dunn, Sternbury, Myer-Briggs, Gardener, Jackson, Kolb, Fleming, and Felder, to name but a few. As stated earlier, the intent of this book is to give you a basic understanding of the key elements of literacy from which you, along with your staff, can pursue additional research in professional literature and on Internet searches. Examining and discussing the elements lead to planning and implementation for school growth. One of the most common models of learning styles is presented for your consideration in Figure 3.2.

DIFFERENTIATED INSTRUCTION

Differentiated instruction is something that all educators should understand. There are students in every classroom, formally identified or not, who can benefit from some sort of differentiation of instruction and assessment. The "one size fits all" approach is being replaced as teachers pay closer attention to the needs of individual students and plan for literacy success for all.

Figures 3.3, 3.4, and 3.5 are materials that will build a deeper understanding of differentiated instruction and can serve, along with the previous material, as the basis for discussion and further investigation. The contents are expressed in generic terms since differentiation should be applied in all learning situations, not just literacy instruction. To focus a discussion on literacy, participants could be asked to use examples about literacy in the dialogue.

These three figures can be used in a number of different approaches. They can be used as a guide for a facilitator in the exploration of materials in a staff meeting, divisional meeting, or professional learning community session. The facilitator could be the principal, a literacy coach, or staff member who has demonstrated some degree of expertise with differentiation. Again, regardless of the role, the presence and participation of the principal plays an important symbolic role.

Figure 3.3 is a list of statements that introduce the topic. They are created to encourage the participants to discuss their understanding of differentiated instruction and dispel myths. It should be stressed that differentiation is diverse and that some or all of

Figure 3.2   Learning Styles

There are three basic learning styles: visual (learning by watching), auditory (learning through listening), and tactile-kinesthetic (learning by doing). Most children start learning through the tactile-kinesthetic modality. The second learning style to develop is visual. The auditory system is last to develop, and researchers believe that it is not fully developed before sixth grade.

VISUAL LEARNING STYLE

- Learn by watching
- Process information by manipulating and forming mental images
- Recall images from the past when remembering and tend to think in pictures
- Need to see the teacher's body language and facial expressions to fully understand the content of a lesson
- Learn best from visual displays such as diagrams, illustrated textbooks, charts, graphs, overhead transparencies, videos, flipcharts, and handouts
- Often prefer to take notes during a classroom discussion

How to recognize a visual learner

Eyes tend to move upward	Neat and orderly	Observant
Memorizes by seeing pictures	Good attention to detail	Has trouble remembering verbal instruction
Cannot fully understand oral directions	Likes to work puzzles	May watch a teacher's face intently

Methods to help visual learners

- Provide a lot of visual directions and demonstrations
- Use matching games, charts, and graphs
- Use color-coded systems
- Retain their attention with pictorial illustrations and a consistent verbal pace

AUDITORY LEARNING STYLE

- Learn through listening
- Interpret the underlying meanings of speech through listening to a person's tone of voice, pitch, speed, and other subtle nuances— written information may have little meaning until it is heard
- Learn through discussions and by listening to what others have to say
- Perform well with spoken directions, discussion groups, and when reading materials out loud

How to recognize an auditory learner		
Steady eyes and body movements	Moves lips and says words when reading	Can remember what was said and can repeat it accurately
Math and writing may be more difficult	Speaks in rhythmic patterns	Learns by listening and talking
Memorizes by steps, procedures, and sequences	Knows all the words to songs	

Methods to help the auditory learner

- Provide him or her with a quiet place to work
- Use the exact wording when repeating information
- Allow them to talk through tasks and think aloud
- Play rhythmic games
- Emphasize verbal repetition
- Have them point to words while reading

TACTILE/KINESTHETIC LEARNING STYLE

- Learn by doing
- Are able to remember and process information by interacting with the physical world around them
- Imperative for kinesthetic learners to be physically involved in what you are teaching
- Learn best by making models of information, breaking information into steps, and incorporating movement while studying

How to recognize a tactile/kinesthetic learner

Responds well to physical rewards	Has difficulty sitting still and is often considered hyperactive	Learns by doing activities and enjoys doing things using hands
Memorizes by walking through each step	Gestures broadly	Responds physically to sensory stimuli
Touches and feels everything	Cannot rote count or sequence materials without aids	Has difficulty understanding the one-to-one relationships between number values and objects

Methods to help the tactile/kinesthetic learner

- Use movement exploration
- Have children clap or tap out numbers and syllables
- Use any and all possible manipulatives
- Provide various activities with 3-D numbers and letters
- Use felt numbers or letters to teach new concepts

the statements could apply. Understanding a student's needs and learning style will determine the best accommodations.

Figure 3.4 takes the understanding and applies it to a chart to help visualize what it would look like in a classroom. The participants could receive the chart with only the left column filled in, and they would complete the right column based on what they have discussed. Alternatively, the two columns could be cut apart, and the task would be to match up and reassemble the chart. Although a relatively simple task, it does encourage reading and thinking about differentiation unlike just distributing materials with the hope that everyone will read and think about it.

Figure 3.5 is a concise guide to differentiation that brings all of the elements together. It reinforces the need for adjusting instruction to meet individual needs and outlines the four elements to be considered in planning for differentiated instruction: learning environment, content, process, and product. It also outlines three areas of focus (readiness, interest, and learning style) and ten easily applied strategies. A valuable activity would be to have the participants in small groups work through the page applying the information to literacy instruction and recording examples. This should be followed by a sharing of the ideas generated by the groups.

Since time constraints could be an issue, the three activities outlined above could be presented at three different times. These could be at three consecutive meetings, perhaps at the beginning of the year. Or they could be at a meeting at the beginning of each term, giving time for reflection and experimentation between sessions. This schedule would also help keep the initiative alive and in the forefront for the year.

You may determine that staff are already knowledgeable about differentiation and are applying the principles and strategies. If this is the case, you may want to use just one of the pieces as a review and reinforcement of differentiated instruction—this can also lead to a sharing of best practices.

Always keep in mind that students learn in their own unique ways. The size of most classes makes individual instruction logistically impossible. Fortunately, there are similarities in student learning styles and needs, so teachers are able to group children appropriately in a variety of ways in the many literacy-learning experiences. Whole-class instruction is sometimes appropriate,

Figure 3.3   What Is Differentiated Instruction?

It has elements from each of the following, as appropriate.

- Differentiated instruction is not just about leveling children by scholastic ability.
  - o It is about matching the academic, social, and emotional needs of students with effective instruction.
- Differentiated instruction is not synonymous with individualized instruction.
  - o If some students are ready for a particular skill, such as using quotation marks, then the teacher provides direct instruction to the students in small groups.
- Differentiated instruction does not mean lines of students waiting for help from the teacher.
  - o When the teacher works with a small group, the other students are working independently or with partners and know that the teacher is temporarily unavailable. After instructing the group, the teacher is again available to help the other students.
- Differentiated instruction does not mean it is hard to keep track of what students know.
  - o Good organization is essential but teachers only need a few good forms to provide them with an overview of what students know and need to know.
- Differentiated instruction is not just about modifying the amount of work students do.
  - o Consider how many examples are needed to demonstrate mastery rather than for practice. Students who finish early should not get more of the same but alternatives that are related to the lesson and allow for extension of learning.
- Differentiation is not just allowing students a choice of learning activity or products to demonstrate learning.
  - o This is one way to differentiate to align with learning style. There are times when the product is the skill (i.e., writing a narrative paragraph where the product is the same for everyone).
- Differentiation in assessment also needs to be used.
  - o Changing a written test to an oral test can make all the difference for some students. Always keep in mind what you are assessing (i.e., a student who has great difficulty printing can still demonstrate an understanding of syllables).

Figure 3.4   A Traditional Classroom Compared to a Differentiated One

Traditional Classroom	Differentiated Classroom
1. Student differences are masked or acted on when problematic.	1. Student differences are studied as a basis for planning.
2. Assessment is most common at the end of learning to see "who got it."	2. Assessment is diagnostic and ongoing to make instruction more responsive to learner needs.
3. A relatively narrow sense of intelligence prevails.	3. Focus on multiple forms of intelligence is evident.
4. A single definition of excellence exists.	4. Excellence is defined in large measure by individual growth from a starting point.
5. Student interest is infrequently tapped.	5. Students are frequently guided in making interest-based learning choices.
6. Relatively few learning profile options are taken into account.	6. Many learning profile options are provided for.
7. Whole-class instruction dominates.	7. Many instructional arrangements are used.
8. Coverage of texts and/or curriculum guides drives instruction.	8. Student readiness, interest, and learning profile shape instruction.
9. Mastery of facts and skills out of context are the focus of learning.	9. Use of essential skills to make sense of/understand key concepts and principles is the focus of learning.
10. Single option assignments are the norm.	10. Multi-option assignments are frequently used.
11. Time is relatively inflexible.	11. Time is used flexibly in accordance with student need.
12. A single text prevails.	12. Multiple materials are provided.
13. Single interpretations of ideas and events may be sought.	13. Multiple perspectives on ideas and events are routinely sought.

14. The teacher directs student behavior.	14. The teacher facilitates students' skills at becoming more self-reliant learners.
15. The teacher solves problems.	15. Students help one another and the teacher solve problems.
16. The teacher provides whole class standards for grading.	16. Students work with the teacher to establish both whole class and individual learning goals.
17. A single form of assessment is often used.	17. Students are assessed in multiple ways.

Figure 3.5   Differentiated Instruction in Action

Four elements need to be considered in planning for differentiated instruction: learning environment, content, process, and product.

Learning environment—the way a classroom feels and functions

- Atmosphere
- Time
- Space
- School and classroom resources
- Effective routines
- Learning supports through charts and models

Content—what we teach and how we give students access to information

- Begin instruction at the students' most appropriate point of entry
- Carefully assess students to determine their prior knowledge, skills, and preferences
- Gather data from a variety of sources, as it is critical to know the whole child

Process—how students come to understand the content

- Consistently use flexible grouping
- Use effective classroom management to adapt instructional delivery to match needs of students
- Adjust for different learning styles, interests, starting points, and abilities

(Continued)

Figure 3.5 (Continued)

Product—how a student demonstrates what he or she has learned

- Conduct initial and ongoing assessment of student readiness and growth
- Encourage students to be active learners—each child should feel challenged most of the time
- Vary expectations and requirements for student responses
- Provide options
- Allow students to work alone or in small groups

There are three areas of focus that enable a teacher to plan for differentiating instruction. It is important for a teacher to know the following:

- The student's *readiness*—refers to the student's starting point in his or her learning (i.e., what the student is bringing to the new learning)
- The student's *interest*—refers to that which interests him or her—what engages the student (i.e., the content or topics that he or she finds relevant and worthwhile)
- The student's *learning style*—refers to how a student learns—this is influenced by learning style, culture, gender

Ten quick and easy differentiation strategies

- Adjust the pacing of instruction
- Build in extra practice
- Provide extra time to complete tasks
- Provide auditory cues (e.g., transitional music or tone)
- Provide visual cues (e.g., anchor charts and use of color and font to highlight information)
- Group and regroup for different purposes
- Vary materials—match texts to readers
- Provide choice
- Build in movement (e.g., demonstrate using actions—a swish of a finger in the air to form an S)
- Start working as a team to identify the resources necessary to support all student needs

---

but more often in literacy, smaller groups are more effective, offering the teacher more opportunity to interact with each child to teach, reinforce, and assess. Although individual instruction may yield excellent results, interacting with their peers gives children practice speaking and listening to others, time for sharing and thinking about diverse ideas, and an opportunity to demonstrate their accomplishments.

SUMMARY

The stages of literacy development, balanced literacy, learning styles, and differentiated instruction work in harmony in meeting the needs of students as they grow in literacy. In a school where there is a common understanding, perhaps through some of the activities presented, students thrive as they move from grade to grade. The continuity created by common practices makes for seamless transitions with shorter adjustment times. Students can more easily carry on from where they left off in the previous year and with a good sense of what literacy experiences to expect and the strategies to employ.

Subsequent chapters will look at ways that the school principal can practice the role of instructional leader by bringing staff together to work through a variety of activities that can establish common literacy values and beliefs. These broader ideas will culminate in the creation of a school improvement plan with a literacy focus. Through the suggested activities, a school can become a vibrant professional learning community where all are honored for what they have to contribute.

CHAPTER 4

Instructional Leadership in Action

The thing always happens that you believe in; and the belief in a thing makes it happen.

—Frank Lloyd Wright, architect

An effective leader is one who reflects on personal performance and then strives to continually improve. Honing leadership skills and practices will help achieve success as an instructional leader by helping the school make the necessary changes to improve literacy achievement for all students. This chapter will help you examine your leadership skills and then offers you the opportunity to put your skills into action, working with staff on the first step to establishing a school literacy improvement plan—establishing common values and beliefs about literacy.

After reading the following quote by Michael Fullan (2003), examine Collins's five-level hierarchy of leadership (as cited in Fullan, 2003) to determine what type of leader you are on the scale (Figure 4.1). Then consider what you will do as you plan to proceed as your school's instructional leader.

Figure 4.1   Collins's Five-Level Hierarchy of Leadership

Level 5: Executive: Builds enduring greatness through a paradoxical blend of personal humility and professional will

Level 4: Effective Leader: Catalyzes commitment to and vigorous pursuit of a clear and compelling vision, stimulating higher performance standards

Level 3: Competent Manager: Organizes people and resources toward the effective and proficient pursuit of predetermined objectives

Level 2: Contributing Team Member: Contributes individual capabilities to the achievement of group objectives and works effectively with others in a group setting

Level 1: Highly Capable Individual: Makes productive contributions through talent, knowledge, skills, and good work habits

SOURCE: Fullan (2003, p. 10).

> The principals we need are level 5 leaders—more like chief operating officers than managers. The teachers we need are immersed in disciplined, informed, professional inquiry and action that results in raising the bar and closing the gap by engaging all students in learning. There is no greater moral imperative than revamping the principal's role as part and parcel of changing the context within which teachers and students learn. (p. 11)

It is in the role of the instructional leader that a school principal will work toward becoming a Level 5 leader. Instructional leadership goes beyond organizing people and resources. It is the ability to inspire others to join in the quest for excellent achievement in literacy for all students while letting credit go to those who have the lion's share of the task, the teachers and students.

Even if the activities in the previous chapters were not used because the teachers in your school already have a very good foundation in literacy because of, perhaps, excellent system level in-servicing, the following activities are designed to inspire discovery and planning that can only happen at the school level. This is when the school principal must step up involvement in the school and grow the role of manager to that of instructional leader.

IDENTIFYING A NEED FOR CHANGE

The principal wants to ensure that the staff and the school community embrace an initiative that will require active involvement by the participants as they review, develop, and implement change. It is acceptance and willingness that will move a plan forward to fruition. To embrace change in literacy instruction, as in any change process, those involved must see and understand the need for change or improvement. Few will expend the time and energy to change just for the sake of changing.

A review of present teaching approaches and resources is required to determine the current state of instruction. Then a gap analysis needs to be made to determine if, for example, there is a discrepancy with school district and state or provincial directives. An examination of school achievement data, especially scores that measure a school to a standard or regional average, should be studied as well. By analyzing the data, a school should be concerned if there is a decline in literacy scores or a stagnant score over a few years. The purpose of the activity is to determine areas for growth and therefore a focus for a literacy growth plan. Even a school with ever-increasing scores can find areas for improvement.

Sometimes, if the requirement to change comes from a non-negotiable source such as a government mandate, the task of review is often considered not necessary and avoided and the "we just have to do it" attitude prevails. To minimize this feeling and to encourage positive participation, data should still be reviewed and discussion initiated. Whatever the circumstances, top down or local choice, success is determined by the degree of understanding of the change by the participants. When there is a universal understanding of why there should be a change, what will change, and the implications and benefits, there is a higher likelihood that the experience will be of benefit to all.

ESTABLISHING A SET OF LITERACY CORE VALUES

Apart from the hard data, an important area to explore is what the principal, teachers, students, and parents believe and understand about literacy (e.g., their roles, instruction, learning, student achievement). These data, generated by a survey or through focus group discussions, may indicate the need to establish a more unified value system. The establishment of clear values and guiding principles that the school will embody is an activity often related to the writing of a vision and mission statement for a school. The process should be a positive experience for everyone; however, it also has the potential to be divisive. It takes active listening, open discussion, acceptance, tolerance, and the willingness of the participants to modify their personal agendas to be successful. The interpersonal skills of the principal will be of great importance to the outcome. Once established, however, a set of values that permeate every aspect of the school makes moving forward much more plausible.

Just as general core values are important for the school, a set of values for a specific area of instruction will help lead the work. If everyone embraces the same values about literacy, implementing strategies across the grades and curricula will happen.

When working toward a common understanding of literacy, initial discussion can be approached in a number of ways. One way would be to open the floor to thoughts. Depending on the staff, this can be very inhibiting as adults are often very self-conscious and hesitant to express personal views openly. It is also too open-ended for many. Another method would be to have small groups of staff work together to discuss and list their understanding of the principles of literacy instruction. Then collectively, the whole staff could collate, analyze, and synthesize their statements. A tool to use for this method is an existing list of guiding principles for teachers to reflect on, and perhaps rank, prior to a discussion (see Figure 4.2). This can activate and give focus to a discussion. To conclude the activity, there needs to be a consensus-building activity. It could be a rank ordering to determine the top statements; it could be the creation of a statement that captures the essence of one or more of the principles; or it could be an agreement that although the school does well in most areas, perhaps there is an area of literacy instruction that needs to be enhanced. The result of the exercise is that the school community shares common values about effective literacy instruction and those will be reflected in literacy instruction and improvement planning. The value statement could even become a school mantra that is posted in the classrooms, halls, and the heading of the school newsletter.

Figure 4.2   Guiding Principles for Literacy

1. Literacy is key to lifelong learning.
2. All students have the right to acquire the literacy skills they need for lifelong learning, and it is the duty of the schools to make this happen.
3. Literacy instruction must be embedded in the curriculum. All teachers of all subjects, from kindergarten to Grade 12, are teachers of literacy.
4. Effective literacy instruction starts with the needs of the learner.
5. Quality literacy instruction for all students enhances the learning of students at risk.
6. All teachers must be equipped with the knowledge and skills to model and teach effective literacy skills in their grade/subject areas.
7. Families and communities must be encouraged and supported in taking action to promote student literacy.
8. Decisions about next steps in literacy for an individual, the school, and the district must be based on a wide range of timely, relevant, and accurate information.
9. Effective literacy learning may require a variety of innovative and flexible structures within the school and community.

An alternative tool (see Figure 4.3) approaches the core values a bit differently. Participants rate the statements using a scale prior to attending the meeting. After collating the responses, the values can be ranked numerically, ready for discussion by the group. The goal is the same as the previous example: establishing core values to direct future developments in literacy instruction.

You may choose to use the Figure 4.2 statements in the same way as the Figure 4.3 statements or vice versa. Only you know what would work best in your school.

A third alternative that can be used with a list of core values or beliefs is called "dotmocracy." Statements from either earlier example are each written on a piece of chart paper. The papers are placed around the room. Each participant is given a sheet of fifteen to twenty colored dots. At the same time, the participants place dots on the statements that they feel most correctly describe what the school presently represents. They may place any number of dots on any of the pages. The activity is then repeated on a new

Figure 4.3   Core Literacy Values

	Agree	Neutral	Disagree
The teaching of reading is the responsibility of every teacher.			
A learner should be treated with respect, even if the learner may be behaving inappropriately.			
A literacy teacher makes a difference in how, what, when, and why students learn.			
Good literacy instruction involves creating as many opportunities as possible for successful learning.			
We must model and then teach strategic literacy skills to our students.			
We will support and encourage each other by teaching literacy skills through mentoring, coaching, sharing, and cooperation.			
Effective two-way communication is the responsibility of every student, teacher, parent, and administrator for literacy success.			
Important literacy initiative decisions must be made collegially.			
Literacy instructional and learning time must be protected.			
We believe that if students work hard, they will achieve success in literacy.			
We have high literacy expectations for every student.			
We have high expectations for ourselves as literacy teachers and administrators.			
We believe that every teacher shares responsibility for the literacy learning of every student in our school.			
We respect, value, and welcome the ideas, input, and concerns of parents about literacy.			

set of pages, with the staff this time placing the dots on what they feel the school should represent. Whether the tally from the two dotmocracies match or differ, the results help lead the discussion and selection of values that will be representative of the school's literacy initiative.

It is expected that only one of the methods explained will be used to establish a common set of literacy values for the school. However, the strategies can be altered and used any time you are collectively trying to come to some sort of agreement on what to choose from a number of possibilities. Using a variety of decision-making methods helps maintain a high interest in the process. Other literacy topics that could be explored are scheduling, record keeping, grouping, homework, and portfolios, to name a few. You need only collectively list the possibilities or issues associated with the topic and then apply one of the strategies to reach agreement. Remember that while the list of possibilities is being developed, there is no discussion because initially you want to get all of the ideas on the table.

Whatever activities are used, the ultimate goal is the establishment of common agreement on literacy that will permeate planning and instruction. With agreement on any aspect, the results should be recorded and distributed. This will not only serve as a reminder but it is a record that can be shared with staff members joining after the literacy initiative has begun. In the future, when decisions need to be made, there will be understanding when the deciding factor between choices is to adopt the one that aligns most closely with the recorded beliefs. "Revisiting what we stand for and questioning the fit between what we believe and what we do is fundamental to any improvement process" (Fullan & St. Germain, 2006, p. 7).

There is a cycle to the process; you should return occasionally to where you began and review the values and practices that have been in place for some time. At least yearly, you should revisit what has been accomplished and the core values. If necessary, consider any new directives that may have been mandated and discoveries made throughout the year. It may be that some core values have changed, or others have become more important. In some areas, this requires changing mission and vision statements for the school. Adjusting is natural, and, as the instructional leader, the principal is instrumental is facilitating the review and revisions.

SUMMARY

Having reached agreement on what the school represents, the next step is to apply the principles to a school improvement or growth plan. A well-developed and articulated plan can provide the catalyst for improvement and the consistency for implementation. The next chapter will lead you through a process and a model for the development of a school growth plan that focuses on literacy. In some school districts, inclusion of literacy is mandated as part of the school improvement plan, or a separate school literacy plan is required. Whatever the case, involving the whole school community in the process will foster ownership and ultimate success. As with previous chapters, many activities and tools are included for the principal to use to facilitate the establishment of a plan.

CHAPTER 5

School Improvement

The Literacy Plan

Well done is better than well said.

—Benjamin Franklin, author, scientist,
inventor, statesman

An integral part of any school growth plan should be a literacy plan. As stated earlier, the school growth plan drives all others and permeates the culture of the school. Depending on where a school is on the continuum of literacy development, a literacy plan focuses everyone on a specific goal or goals. It could be a plan in which a school is just beginning to make a serious commitment to literacy, and the plan needs to emphasize teacher professional growth and experimentation with strategies in the classrooms. With trained staff, ongoing professional growth is still important, but the plan may focus on full implementation of classroom practices and on putting a process in place to ensure that effective literacy instruction is being used in all classrooms. The next step could then be to focus on assessment practices, uses, and implications.

Whatever stage a school is at, caution should be taken that the plan does not encompass more than is possible to achieve in a given time period. A plan with many goals and unrealistic time requirements can be overwhelming and counterproductive. Yearly plans, for this reason, have given way to multiyear plans in which the pace is managed by setting benchmark goals. The final goals may require a number of years to achieve. "It takes 3 to 5 years for complex changes to move from initiation to institutionalization" (Fullan, 1991, cited in Munger, 2006).

There is little doubt that student achievement in literacy will affect achievement in all subject areas and that school improvement plans need to embed literacy into the initiatives. In order to take an objective look at how successful literacy instruction is at a school, data on achievement levels in standardized tests, system level tests, and classroom performance are required. Although the demographics of a school play a role, effective instruction is the key to student success. There are many examples of demographically disadvantaged schools that, through school growth plans focused on improving instruction, have been able to greatly improve student literacy success. Increasingly, data-directed decisions are leading to mutually agreed-on actions and the expected measurable outcomes are then articulated in improvement plans. Revisiting the plan regularly at staff meetings by looking at new data, the initiatives are kept at the forefront.

Chapter 7 offers a number of models and activities that lead a school in the creation of a viable literacy growth plan to improve student achievement. Throughout the process, it is beneficial to remind staff that the literacy plan is not a separate entity but rather the foundation for the other planning that occurs, such as daily plans, long-range plans, division or grade plans, and teacher professional growth plans. The alignment of all of these plans indicates that the literacy plan is entrenched in the daily activities in the school, and staff will realize that working toward the goals in one plan will also achieve the goals in the others.

DEVELOPING A LITERACY PLAN

The development of a literacy plan requires consideration of the following elements that are common to many planning models:

Gathering and analyzing data

Review of current practices and resources

Brainstorming and researching alternatives

Consensus building

Articulation of a plan that includes clear goals, expected outcomes, responsibilities, timelines, financial considerations, and methods to measure progress

Promotion of the plan

Implementation of the plan

Monitoring of progress

Review of progress

Making recommendations for future developments

The desire, skill, and knowledge of a principal will impact the successful navigation of a staff through these elements. Skilled principals are able to motivate staff and see the plan successfully to its conclusion and then build on it, facilitating the creation of subsequent plans. Good leadership is the key to the success of the process. This is not to imply a top-down model but rather an emphasis on the supportive role that a principal plays. The value that a principal places on a literacy plan, the effort the principal expends to facilitate the development and expedition of the plan, the financial and resource support made available, and the continued interest in the progress of the plan all contribute to the success. Without a support base such as this, even the most dedicated staff may have difficulty staying the course and improving instruction consistently across the school. Substantial improvement in instruction may happen even in schools lacking strong leadership, but this improvement is often due only to the individual initiative of the teacher. For literacy to become truly embedded in the culture of the school, effective instructional leadership is required.

Understanding the School

It is common for principals to be transferred from school to school on a regular cycle. Teachers, on the other hand, may be at only a few schools in their entire career. An incoming principal will be stepping into a school that may or may not have an established culture of effective literacy instruction. Although the previous principal will offer an opinion of the progress of the school, hopefully with supporting data, the incoming principal needs to establish his or her own level of understanding of the school and belief about literacy.

An effective tool to use, and one that is especially beneficial with a staff just beginning the process of establishing a literacy plan, is a gathering of thoughts based on the questions in Figure 5.1. The activity requires the staff to reflect on what an ideal literate school would be like. The purpose of the activity is to establish a set of common beliefs that, combined with values established in earlier activities, can be used as a focus for school growth planning. The questions are written on the top of chart paper, one question per page. Participants, in groups, are assigned one of the questions and they record their answers.

Once a list of responses for each question has been generated, discuss the results. Look for common statements and work to develop a list of agreed-on beliefs. These beliefs about exceptional practices give the staff a standard from which to do a gap analysis of current practice in the school and to make plans to address identified areas of need. This valuable exercise may take more than one session. Individuals may need time to think about the discussion prior to the creation of a set of literacy beliefs that they know will define the school's culture and influence future decisions and practices.

Figure 5.1   What Does a Literate School Look Like?

Reflective Questions

1. What are the teachers in a literate school doing?

2. What are students doing in a literate school?

3. What is the principal doing in a literate school?

4. What does the physical building look like?

5. How does the community support a literate school?

Figure 5.2 is an example of what the completed charts may include and can vary greatly from the actual list generated at the session due to the participants' understanding of literacy instruction. The ideas shared here are many of the common responses to the activity and not presented in any particular order of importance. They are included to help the activity leader (likely, but not necessarily, the principal) and offer additional ideas during the

Figure 5.2   What Does a Literate School Look Like? Sample Responses

---

1. **What are the teachers in a literate school doing?**

   - Actively engage students
   - Use strategic instruction
   - Use assessment based program and delivery
   - Implement effective scheduling and planning
   - Model good learning strategies
   - Engage in professional discussions in the staff room
   - Work together partnering or in teams of teachers
   - Share materials and ideas
   - Are excited about student learning
   - Activate prior knowledge to connect students to learning
   - State purpose for learning/assignments
   - Ensure all students are engaged
   - Ask questions that promote higher order thinking skills
   - Develop curiosity in students
   - Offer students some choice in what they are doing and input into rubric for assessment
   - Explicitly teach learning processes
   - Deliver a balanced program
   - Are invitational to parents

2. **What are students doing in a literate school?**

   - Actively engaged in learning with minimal wiggle time or standing in line waiting for the teacher
   - Ask good questions
   - Work toward independence
   - Complete culminating activities and performance tasks
   - Can articulate their learning
   - Make connections between and across curriculum areas
   - Use graphic organizers, apply vocabulary, read, write, and so on, together and on their own
   - Expand and apply literacy skills

(Continued)

Figure 5.2 (Continued)

- Share their accomplishments with each other
- Gain confidence in themselves
- Progress at an appropriate rate for individual abilities

3. **What is the principal doing in a literate school?**
   - Is seen leading and challenging staff and students to grow
   - Provides resources, both material and human
   - Demonstrates a commitment to literacy by making it a priority
   - Visits classrooms to watch for "look fors"
   - Maintains a positive attitude
   - Encourages and supports staff and students
   - Creates release time for teachers and teams of teachers
   - Communicates the vision to all: students, staff, parents, and community
   - Defines and articulates baseline and expectations to achieve a vision
   - Facilitates collegial decision making
   - Encourages effective two-way communication
   - Attends staff development sessions with staff when possible
   - Incorporates staff development and sharing into staff meetings
   - Creates timetables to facilitate shared preparation time for teams
   - Creates timetables for uninterrupted time for language arts instruction
   - Provides opportunities for inexperienced teachers to visit mentor-teacher classrooms
   - Maintains communication with literacy support teachers
   - Facilitates the development of centrally organized literacy materials for effective sharing (e.g., leveled book room)

4. **What does the physical building look like?**
   - Volunteers helping in the classroom with tasks such as listening to children read, helping them write, reinforcing language skills, and managing home reading programs
   - Evidence of students' work in literacy prominently displayed
   - Wealth of environment print (e.g., word walls, reference charts)
   - Assessment tools and tracking charts displayed in staff workrooms
   - Library used frequently
   - Evidence of student pride in risk taking and accomplishments

5. **How does the community support a literate school?**
   - Involvement of parent groups in a school council/parent/teacher association
   - Parents supporting children at home in home reading programs
   - Volunteers in the classrooms
   - Donations of books and materials
   - Fund-raising to purchase materials to support events such as author visits
   - Attendance at literacy information events
   - Business community sponsorships

discussion. Once again, if the principal is not the activity facilitator, the principal's participation as a group member is important because it supports the value of professional development in literacy.

Understanding the Teachers and Yourself

A principal must also ascertain the resources in the school, in particular the human resources. Again the previous principal can be a great source of information, but whether a principal assesses the human resource through referral or from working with the staff for a period of time, it is to the school leader's advantage to determine which staff members are most likely to be the most influential in facilitating literacy growth in the school.

On any staff, there is a wide range of abilities and personalities. There are staff members who see change in literacy instruction as an exciting opportunity and those who resist any kind of change and are satisfied with their present practices. Some will take on an initiative and make it their own, exceeding every expectation, while others will work to sabotage progress. There are some staff who, given enough information and indicators of success in another class, will more willingly work toward implementing the literacy plan. Knowing the traits of the individual staff members and having the skill to work positively with each is a challenge for every principal. It is unrealistic to believe that everyone will embrace change in the same way. A principal who knows how to get the best out of each member on staff will have more success as an instructional leader.

Many models can be used when considering the needs and willingness of staff in the change process. Hall and Hord's (2001) Concerns-Based Adoption Model (Figure 5.3) is useful in considering an individual staff member's attitude toward a literacy initiative. Another approach is to use a scale that considers reaction to change such as Rogers's (1995) Individual Innovativeness Theory as seen in Figure 5.4. Understanding where each staff member fits on a scale as well as the needs of the individuals at that level can help the principal decide what can be done to help those who appear to be resistors become more receptive to change. Sometimes it can be a simple matter of supplying more information, examples, and time to digest the materials.

Figure 5.3   Concerns-Based Adoption Model (CBAM)

Stages of Concern About Innovation

6. **Refocusing:** The focus is on the exploration of more universal benefits from the innovation, including the possibility of major changes or replacement with a more powerful alternative. Individual has definite ideas about alternatives to the proposed or existing form of the innovation.

5. **Collaboration:** The focus is on coordination and cooperation with others regarding use of the innovation.

4. **Consequences:** Attention focuses on impact of the innovation on students in his/her immediate sphere of influence. The focus is on relevance of the innovation for students, evaluation of outcomes including performance and competencies, and changes needed to increase outcomes.

3. **Management:** Attention is focused on the processes and tasks of using the innovation and the best use of information and resources. Issues related to efficiency, organization, management, scheduling, and time demands are of utmost importance.

2. **Personal:** Individual is uncertain about the demands of the innovation, his/her inadequacy to meet those demands, and his/her role in the innovation. This includes analysis of his/her role in relation to the structure of the organization, decision making, and consideration of potential conflicts with existing structures or personal commitment. Financial or status implications of the program for self and colleagues may also be reflected.

1. **Informational:** A general awareness of the innovation and interest in learning more detail about it is indicated. The person seems to be unworried about himself/herself in relation to the innovation. He/she is interested in substantive aspects of the innovation in a selfless manner, such as general characteristics, effects, and requirements for use.

0. **Awareness:** Little concern about or involvement with the innovation is indicated.

SOURCE: Hall and Hord (2001).

Some caution must be taken with these models. They present generalities and few individuals neatly fit into a single category. Each school staff is different, and in a small staff, all categories may not be represented. There are other models, True Colors (www.true-colors.com), for example, but they all have the same purpose: enhancing the understanding of different reactions to

Figure 5.4   Individual Innovativeness Scale

Innovators—the risk takers willing to take the initiative and time to try something new (generally 2.5% of the participants)

Early adopters—tend to be respected group leaders; the individuals essential to adoption by the whole group (about 13.5% of the participants)

Early majority—the careful, safe, deliberate individuals unwilling to risk time or other resources (about 34% of the participants)

Late majority—those suspect of or resistant to change; hard to move without significant influence (about 34% of the participants)

Laggards—those who are consistent or even adamant in resting change; pressure needed to force change (about 16% of the participants)

SOURCE: Rogers (1995).

NOTE: Percentages are estimates and vary slightly in similar models.

change that should be considered when choosing methods to unify the staff in order to achieve a common goal—in this instance, effective literacy instruction. Keeping the emotional needs of the individual teachers in mind, you can avoid alienating some from the initiative and monopolize on the contributing factors. Knowing what individuals require and when they are ready to move forward will help you help each staff member develop at his or her own pace.

Once a principal understands the staff, the question is this: As a school develops and moves forward with a literacy plan, to which individuals should a principal give the most time, energy, and resources? According to Todd Whittaker (2003), the answer is not to those that require the most change. To get them to accept and adopt change can be a long and frustrating task. Those individuals who will accept the support of the principal, who are willing to take some risk, and who will serve as role models for the others will make the difference. Their successes will be the inspiration for the others who need the reassurance that change in literacy instruction will lead to increased student achievement.

Whittaker (2003), in *What Great Principals Do Differently*, categorizes teachers as *superstars*, *backbones*, or *mediocres*. He suggests that a principal base decisions on the best teachers, the superstars. If a superstar endorses a decision, it is very likely a good one. He says a superstar is a teacher who (1) former students remember as their best teacher, (2) parents regularly request for their children, (3) peers respect, and (4) would probably be difficult to replace if he or she leaves the school. Superstars are rare, and often a school only has one or two, but they are the individuals who will move literacy forward.

Principals should not forget to reflect on their own strengths and weaknesses as well. Determine where you fit in using the same tools applied to the staff. This could be a revelation as to why you have had more success with some staff than others. If, for example, you are an innovator, you may tend to charge ahead, forgetting that others need more reassurance and understanding of why changes must occur.

You may also consider other popular instruments such as the Bar-On Emotional Quotient Inventory, EQ-i, developed by Reuven Bar-On, PhD (www.reuvenbaron.org) by which individuals learn about themselves and how they best work with others. After the questionnaire is completed, the professionally tabulated scores indicate emotional and social areas of strength and needs. The report makes suggestions for improvement and how to avoid letting your strengths adversely affect interaction with others. A principal who realizes and understands what in his or her style and personality inspires or distances others can use the information to plan effectively for growth. For example, a principal who finds it difficult to empathize with others will likely not appreciate the strain and frustration in staff members who find change to be threatening. Realizing this weakness, the principal should depend on the help of trusted staff members to monitor the emotional pulse in the school and heed their advice to slow down the pace and give the staff time to learn about literacy instructional strategies. They can then take action to help alleviate the angst by perhaps altering timelines or arranging for outside in-service assistance.

Another important example: A principal who has the ability to trust others will find it easier to share the leadership in a school and be able to delegate responsibilities to others. This strategy ensures ownership of a literacy initiative by many of the staff and, in turn, successful implementation. Principals lacking trust tend to do it all themselves, making the initiative personal rather than collective and collaborative. This type of approach rarely inspires others. By focusing on personal strengths and adjusting for weaknesses, effective leaders can cause change and growth to occur.

PLANNING FOR LITERACY INSTRUCTION

Creating a literacy plan requires the principal and staff to determine what tasks need to be accomplished and to have a clear understanding of everyone's role in moving literacy instruction forward. The list of reflective questions in Figure 5.5 is designed to promote discussion and inspire the making of collegial plans. A principal, as facilitator, may select the questions that are most pertinent to the school or use a strategy such as dotmocracy, described in Chapter 4, with the staff to determine what issue they would like to focus on. Some schools may have a clear set of established beliefs but need to focus on implementation; another school may have a well-established program but

Figure 5.5   Reflecting on the Literacy Program

1. What are our beliefs about literacy?

2. What are the roles of the principal, teachers, students, and parents in literacy?

3. What does it mean to implement a research-based literacy program?

4. How do we ensure the purposeful use of a literacy block?

5. What are the school's goals for literacy?

6. How do we assess student literacy progress and how do the results direct instruction?

7. Do we have adequate instructional resources?

8. Are resources being used effectively?

9. How engaged are we in the literacy initiative?

10. How can we enhance home–school connections?

11. What supports are provided to the principal and teachers in the literacy initiative?

12. How can we maintain the initiative and help each other along?

is concerned about assessment. The selected questions serve to focus discussion with the aim of establishing literacy goals.

As a question is discussed, many other important questions may arise: Is this reflective of reality or idealistic? How can the school move in that direction? What are the logistical and financial implications? Are the solutions the best for the students? Who needs to be involved and with what responsibilities? Does this align with curriculum mandates? What is the school district direction? The discussion can be intense and it will take a skilled leader to control and guide it to a favorable conclusion.

Also remember that staff, working together, should be encouraged to look for answers from a number of different sources: literature, data, and district-level personnel. The consolidation of information and open discussion of the data are key to ownership and the ensuing success of a literacy initiative.

If all the questions are to be discussed, the activity cannot be completed at one meeting because that would be overwhelming. Select a few questions for each discussion period. The range is very wide, and there is room for debate, fact finding, and decision making in each question. Some questions can be answered quickly, since some structures are likely in place. Regardless, it is important to determine if unity exists and identify the need and focus for change.

The school review chart (Figure 5.6) is another example guide for specific inquiry into the existing attributes of a school that affect student progress. Remember that this is an important step in the planning process because it helps ensure continuity between yearly plans, and it reviews successful methods. After careful consideration and discussion of the questions, the staff will be ready to move to the next step of articulating the plan in a format such as one presented later in the book.

After establishing literacy values and goals, taking a close look at literacy instruction as it exists, understanding the strengths and needs of the personnel involved, and reviewing previous literacy improvement initiatives, the next step is to create an action plan to improve literacy instruction. The collaborative activity of putting a plan together will help staff take ownership, which is critical to the success of the plan. Choosing to focus on only a few goals at a time is wise. A school with too many goals gets lost in the initiatives, accomplishing little of each and seeing few to conclusion. With few goals, all energy and resources can be directed

Figure 5.6 School Review

Data	Goals	Strategies	Resources	Monitoring
Review of • Provincial/ state scores • Standardized test scores • Report card scores • Staff survey • Parent survey • School facilities survey	Review • Previous goals and progress notes Ask • Were they accomplished? • What has yet to be addressed? • How realistic were they? • What changes were made as we worked through the plan?	Ask • What strategies were most successful in reaching goals and why? • What strategies were not effective and why?	Determine • What resources were utilized and how effective were they? • What resources will be available (e.g., human, facility, financial, system)?	Ask • Was monitoring ongoing, collaborative, and focused? • Did the methods obtain the information needed?

71

properly and results are readily evident. The adage "do a few things well rather than many poorly" certainly applies to a school literacy plan. By concentrating time and energy on a few goals, results can become apparent more quickly. The momentum to continue is often determined by the degree that there is perceived progress.

By developing and articulating a schoolwide literacy plan, it is made clear to everyone what has to be done, how, by whom, by when, and with what supports. A good strategy is to begin the write-up of the plan with the values and belief statements created earlier. This will remind the staff of decisions that were made and serve as a reference for the contents of the literacy plan. Many school districts have adopted a form of school improvement or growth plan structured similar to Figure 5.7. The sample plan is for developing a leveled book room for a school as one literacy goal. The structure remains the same for each goal in the plan. A structure such as this can be used with even the smallest of plans. The plan helps keep an initiative on track and allows for shared leadership. Revisiting the plan regularly and maintaining progress notes helps keep the plan alive and support it to fruition.

It cannot be stressed enough that staff members should be actively involved in the content of the plan. If they help establish the goals, determine the strategies, take on some responsibilities, and choose resources, they are more likely to strive for success to the point of going beyond expectations.

SMART Goals

The setting of goals or targets gives a literacy plan clear purpose. Staying the course to a known goal or goals keeps a school from being sidetracked. When a new directive comes along, a school with a plan firmly in place knows how much more can be taken on and when to defer action if possible. There can be a tendency to react and take on more than is humanly possible when there is not a clear picture of what the school is already working toward. Stress, uncertainty, and poorly implemented changes will be the result in a school without a plan.

Recently, school systems have encouraged the use of numeric targets to further define goals. SMART goals, first coined by Peter Drucker in *The Practice of Management* (1954), have become popular. There are many versions of this model as school systems modify it to reflect local practices. The goal in Figure 5.8 is just an

Figure 5.7 School Growth Plan

Goal	To establish a leveled book room of leveled literacy materials for Grades 1 through 3 with at least two resources at each of the Fountas and Pinnell (1999) instructional levels by June of this school year
Strategies	• Visit existing leveled book rooms at other schools to view examples • Research publishers for materials to include • Determine structure and format for room • Collect and collate existing materials • Determine and order desired materials • Set up room • Arrange for release time for lead teacher • In-service teacher regarding contents and use of resources
Responsibilities	• Visits—lead teacher, principal • Research—teachers • Collection—teachers • Collate—leveled book room lead teacher • Structure—lead teacher, teachers, principal • Setup—lead teacher • Release time—principal • In-service—lead teacher
Resources	• Various publishing company catalogues • Presentations by publishing company representatives • Existing materials • System staff for guidance on book rooms and in-servicing on shared and guided reading
Budget	Occasional teacher to release staff member to work on project $——— times 19 release days Materials $1,000.00 Books $3,000.00
Timeline	September—visits to other sites October—establish structure/research materials November—order resources January through March—set up room April—in-service May through June—pilot use June—evaluation of resource and future planning Following year—full implementation
Progress notes	

Figure 5.8   SMART Goals

SMART goals are
 	
    Strategic and specific
 	
    Measurable, meaningful, and monitored
 	
    Attainable and action-oriented
 	
    Results-oriented and relevant
 	
    Time-bound and tracked

example. Some versions add an E for Exciting and Evaluated and an R for Recorded, Rewarding, and Reviewed, making them SMARTER goals. Some words are only other ways to express terms found elsewhere in the acronym, so careful selection is required before using a version to write targets in order to avoid confusion. Prior to writing SMART goals, it is suggested that some training occur because it is a precise skill.

The example goal in Figure 5.7 has SMART goal qualities. The leveled book room is a strategic literacy move for a school, and the grade span and type of materials are specific. The number of books is measurable, the resource has meaning to the program, and the progress can be monitored for quality and for any adjustment as required. The budget and amount of material needed makes the goal attainable, and there is a definite action required to achieve the goal. The use of the materials from the book room in the classroom is aimed at improving literacy results, and it is relevant to the literacy initiative. There is a timeline, and the progress can be tracked, in this case for expenditures.

Goals can also be expressed in terms of student achievement. Here is an example: Ninety percent of the students in Grade 3 will achieve Level 3 or better in reading as measured by the Education Quality and Accountability Office (EQAO) Ontario provincial assessment in the 2008 school year.

The wording of this goal also meets with the required criteria.

For training purposes, the two examples could be analyzed by a group of teachers as an exercise to help everyone understand how to construct SMART goals prior to writing targeted goals for the school literacy plan.

The Senior School Challenge

Building a literacy plan in a senior school has unique challenges. The size of the staff, the specialization of the teachers, and the division of subjects into classes for students combine to increase the challenge of raising literacy scores. A staff must first understand the importance of addressing literacy across the curriculum and accept that it is the responsibility of all teachers, regardless of discipline, to help students become more literate. The science teacher, for example, needs to understand that a science textbook is quite different from a history text and that students may need specific instruction to get the most out of reading scientific texts. Teachers in each subject must look at the different structures of their texts and realize that understanding how to glean information from the different structures is possibly not covered in English classes. The application of English composition and presentation skills must also be a shared responsibility. Students benefit from a cross-curricular approach to teaching literacy as they see the application of knowledge and skills learned in one discipline being applied in another. The ability to consolidate and apply skills will help students achieve better results in even their weakest subjects. Once there is an understanding and acceptance of this philosophy, a literacy initiative in a senior school can be very successful. Even if all staff do not agree initially, once initiated, student success in participating classes will confirm the impact that can be made by every teacher sharing in literacy instruction.

The following successful strategies have proven to be helpful in raising literacy scores in senior schools:

> Make the improvement of literacy scores a whole-school goal. As a principal, deliver that message. Ensure that all subject areas make this a part of their planning and develop a content-based rather than a test-based approach to literacy.

> Analyze state and provincial test results to identify and address specific areas of concern rather than set general goals (e.g., students experience difficulty making connections between personal knowledge and experiences and ideas and information in the reading selections).

> Present data to all staff to support these concerns.

Model, teach, and ensure that the staff has the knowledge of research-based strategies that target the specific areas of concern. Use a variety of venues to assist teachers (e.g., staff meetings, in-service, department meetings, roundtables, and readings). Make sure the strategies reflect application to a variety of subject disciplines and be sure to show how these strategies improve learning.

Have subject areas develop tasks and summative assessments that reflect the tasks demanded on the literacy test. Have subject areas share their strategies. Use the performance appraisal process to support literacy as a whole school goal.

Offer after-school literacy programs.

Link with the parent community through information nights and the selling of resources (e.g., workbooks, CDs).

Continue to use data to celebrate areas of improvement and growth.

Reading through the list, it can be agreed that some of these strategies also apply to elementary schools just as earlier strategies for working with staff apply to senior school settings. Regardless, there is no doubt that the use of mutually developed school improvement plans that incorporate literacy helps maintain focus for a school and leads to literacy success.

SUMMARY

A well-articulated, collaborative literacy plan based on the values and beliefs of the school and the curriculum requirements that also has the obvious support of an encouraging administration is destined for success. This chapter has offered many tools to use to accomplish this task, beginning with understanding the school and the staff. Writing SMART goals and defining each aspect of the plan is important because it gives the staff a clear vision of what is to be accomplished and how that can happen. Writing a plan, however, is just an exercise; implementing the plan, monitoring the progress, and modifying as needed are all required to realize results.

It is important to keep the momentum going in a literacy improvement plan. This can be done in a number of ways by the principal: staging events that celebrate the successes, including progress updates and discussion of the literacy plan as a regular item on staff and divisional meeting agendas, facilitating sharing between teachers and between schools, allocating funds to support the plan, including items about the progress in school newsletters, involving the parent council, participating with staff at in-service sessions, and sharing in the tasks identified to support the plan. No doubt there are many more ideas, but the point is made: An involved principal contributes greatly to the success of a plan for improvement in literacy instruction and achievement.

The remaining chapters address how the school literacy plan can be successfully supported and implemented. Although seemingly separate topics, they must be viewed as components that work together as they share a common element: working together. The variety of combinations of partnerships complement each other as they work in harmony to achieve the literacy plan. Without each of these combinations, success will be more difficult to achieve. The partnerships include staff and parents, shared leadership by the principal and staff, teams of teachers, and the principal's support of individual teachers in classroom instruction.

CHAPTER 6

Working Together

Promoting Home/School/ Community Partnerships

Alone we can do so little; together we can do so much.

—Helen Keller, author and activist

Family involvement in a child's education is a more important factor in student success than family income or education.

—International Reading Association (2002)

The value of the support from the home and community cannot be overstated. Children in homes where reading is modeled and encouraged come to school primed for literacy success. Community members who interact with the school also model for the students what having a good education, literacy skills in particular, can mean to their futures. Fostering these relationships is an investment for the school and an achievement for the students. Although teachers may create a bond between themselves and the parents of the children in their present class, the promotion of the whole school and, precisely for literacy, sharing an understanding of literacy instruction with the community generally requires facilitation by the principal. As the instructional leader, building and maintaining the connections is important. Schools should always remember that regardless of the level of involvement of parents and the community, this link must be nurtured, input respected, and interactions celebrated.

UNDERSTANDING THE SCHOOL COMMUNITY

In some areas, the involvement of the home and community seems to be a natural occurrence, in others it must be worked on. Many factors contribute to the level and type of connection that exists. When discussing with the staff what can be done to strengthen or expand the connection, consider these aspects:

Existing relationship—What is perceived as the present relationship between the school and the community? A survey of the parents, students, and staff could help determine the perceptions.

Transient rate—Does the school have a stable student base, or is there a high degree of movement of families in and out of the community? These data are easily accessed from the student database used at the school. How are new families welcomed to the school? Are there orientation materials? With a high transient rate, what measures are in place to alleviate stress on the parents, students, and teachers?

Socioeconomic status—Areas of lower-income families have been traditionally perceived as those that also have lower literacy scores partially due to limited parental involvement. What is being done to keep literacy scores high? What measures are being taken to involve the parents?

Ethnic/cultural backgrounds—Understand the ethnic background of the community. Some cultures traditionally do not question or become involved with education. Does the school acknowledge the differences in cultures and make accommodations to respect the differences? How are these parents encouraged to become involved? Are there measures in place so that information goes home in appropriate languages?

Volunteer base—Does the school enjoy a large volunteer base? What tasks do the volunteers perform? Are the tasks clerical, supervisory, or instructional? Do the tasks give the volunteers an opportunity to help literacy development in students? Do volunteers feel that they make a meaningful contribution? A poll of teachers and volunteers can quickly collect these data.

Atmosphere in the school—Does the school project an inviting atmosphere? Is it physically attractive and maintained? How are guests greeted and treated? Is there a positive feeling? Ask the visitors and find out!

School Parent Council involvement—What is on the School Parent Council agenda? Does it often contain issues of concern and information about ongoing initiatives such as literacy? Are the meetings well attended? If not, why? Are members of the group often in the school during instructional hours? Are requests from teachers well received? Do they feel valued and involved in decisions made at the school? Principal and staff discussion with the group will help answer these questions.

Teacher attitudes—How do the teachers feel about themselves? Are they happy to be there? Do they feel valued? Do they feel they have a voice in making decisions at staff meetings? Do they feel overloaded? How do they approach issues with parents? Are issues resolved positively? Do they feel supported by the principal in parent issues? Some of these are more difficult to get answers to. Success depends on the relationship with the principal and the ability to have open discussion.

Student attitudes—Do students feel safe at school? Do they like being there? Do they feel valued? Are they listened to? Do they trust the staff and the principal? Do they feel successful? An anonymous student survey could help determine the answers to these questions.

Existing connections—Is there a school newsletter? What type of information does it contain? How often is it sent home? Is there something that encourages parents to read it? Are there monthly class newsletters sent home by the teachers informing parents of the focus for instruction, literacy, and so on, with suggestions for ways they can help their children? How often are parents invited into the school for interviews and conferences? Do teachers phone parents? Are these interactions both to praise achievement and for problem solving?

Suggestions—Does the school have a suggestion box or a process to receive suggestions and concerns? How are the suggestions received? Is there communication about why a suggestion can or cannot be honored?

This list is extensive but certainly not all-inclusive. There may be other factors worth investigating unique to a school and other questions that need to be posed. Whatever aspects a school chooses to investigate with a fact-finding exercise, the results can be used to increase and promote positive connections. These connections can then be used to help promote an understanding of a school's literacy program and encourage parent involvement.

ANALYZING THE DATA

After completing the fact finding, the next step is to analyze the data. Find out what is and what is not working. A valuable activity is to take the results and sort them into contributing or inhibiting factors. The contributing factors need to be celebrated and enhanced. By bringing them to the forefront, everyone begins to appreciate the bond between the parents and the school. The inhibiting factors, however, are not to be ignored. They need to be resolved in a caring, collaborative way. Depending on the urgency of the issues, it is far more effective to resolve them one at a time rather than trying to do everything at once. It may even be discovered that the resolution of one issue has a positive affect on another, either resolving the second issue or making it more manageable. Parents and a community seeing a school acknowledge and address issues that affect the literacy success of their students cannot help but become more supportive.

Collecting and analyzing the data, however difficult that may be, is well worth the effort. Sometimes even the most apparently insignificant piece of information, used effectively, can reap positive results. For example, in a school, the results of a student survey on reading preferences and habits indicated that many students liked to listen to music while reading. Contrary to popular belief that a quiet surrounding is the best way to concentrate on what a person is reading, the intermediate division of the school experimented with playing music during "drop everything and read" time. To test the success of the experiment, students used the reading time to read stories that were also discussed in literature circles. Many students found the addition of music both enjoyable and beneficial. The quality of discussion in their groups indicated no sign that music adversely affected reading. In fact, some students were better prepared for the discussion. Of course, there were students who found the music distracting, so accommodations were made to satisfy both groups. This information, shared with parents, helped eliminate battles at home over whether students must study without any distracting sound. The benefits of this observation were appreciated by both parents and students and helped enhance the home connection, making future recommendations more easily accepted.

Communication with the home and community is a critical element that contributes to positive connections. Newsletters from both the school and the classroom keep parents informed about literacy expectations. Suggestions for support of learning at home such as letter writing, family book nights, and storytelling should be included. Report cards and parent–teacher interviews help parents understand and support the academic growth of their child. Holding a literacy evening, a chance for parents to come to the school for a presentation on literacy development, is another tried-and-true strategy. Even if the turnout is small, the attending parents appreciate the information. The subsequent event may have even better attendance as word spreads about the value of the evening. Reporting on developments in the literacy program at the Parent Teacher Association or School Advisory Group meetings further enhances the parents' understanding and support of literacy initiatives. Home reading programs have children taking books home and practicing specific reading strategies. As the parent listens to the child and helps him or her master the accompanying strategy card, the parent learns how to help his or her own child become a better reader with other reading material. Another welcome piece of information that parents appreciate is a flyer or list of generic suggestions about what they can do to help develop literacy in their child at home over the summer months. Whatever methods are used, and there are many different possibilities, effective communication with the home serves to cement the relationship.

In a community-connected school, the parents know and appreciate the efforts and genuine concern of the teachers, and they are generally more willing to help out at home. A good working relationship with the home allows the school to make suggestions to the parents. After sharing a student's literacy needs with parents, a teacher suggests that reading to the child each night is very important. Because of the reputation of the school and the degree of trust established, the parents understand, appreciate, and act on the request. The same parents can be invited to help with a home reading program. This offers them the opportunity to see literacy skills in action, and since the school is seen as a welcoming place, they feel comfortable accepting the offer. This scenario, although seemingly idealistic, is being played out in successful schools across the continent.

Academic achievement is enhanced when a school has good rapport and a working relationship with the home. When the home places importance on literacy, the child more easily understands and embraces a school with a culture of literacy.

SUMMARY

Partnerships are very important in education. Working with parents and the community has the potential for a great impact on student success. The key component in this partnership is open communication. Maintaining transparency, mutual respect, honesty, and integrity, even in difficult times, can result in a successful working relationship with students at the core.

The partnerships within a school have a similar effect, particularly those in which a principal shares the leadership of the literacy initiative with staff who are well versed and experienced in the field. The next chapter will explore shared leadership, the paradigm shift from traditional leadership, and how it enhances the implementation of the school plan for increased achievement in literacy.

CHAPTER 7

Sharing Leadership

No man will make a great leader who wants to do it all himself, or to get all the credit for doing it.

—Andrew Carnegie, industrialist, businessman, and philanthropist

The age in which the principal was viewed as a superbeing who can do it all and does it all is long gone. A number of factors have contributed to a changed image of the role of the principal. The increased demands on time, the vast array of tasks to accomplish, and the need to keep up with rapid curriculum development have made it impossible to maintain this superbeing status. With an increased understanding of ownership and its value in the success of an initiative, top-down leadership has proven to be one of the least effective methods of implementing change.

There has been a shift in the traditional hierarchical structure of schools. Teachers, at one time, were expected to adopt new curriculum and teaching strategies with few options and little opportunity to discuss and resolve issues. Top-down leadership did little to actively involve teachers in the decision-making process. Recently, there is more value placed on teachers with expertise in a field that will enhance the school as a whole. There is now a better understanding of the power of teamwork and collegial decision making,

Figure 7.1   Classical and Shared Leadership

Classical Leadership	Shared Leadership
Displayed by a person's position in a group or hierarchy.	Identified by the quality of people's interactions rather than their position.
Leadership evaluated by whether the leader solves problems.	Leadership evaluated by how people are working together.
Leaders provide solutions and answers.	All work together to enhance the process and to make it more fulfilling.
Distinct differences between leaders and followers: character, skill, etc.	People are interdependent. All are active participants in the process of leadership.
Communication is often formal.	Communication is crucial with a stress on conversation.
Can often rely on secrecy, deception, and payoffs.	Values democratic processes, honesty, and shared ethics. Seeks a common good.

SOURCE: Doyle and Smith (2001).

which has proven to be far more productive. We have moved to an era of shared leadership that has many and sometimes unexpected benefits. The current development of vibrant and productive professional learning communities in schools and between schools attests to the success of the shift of responsibility.

Shared leadership involves individuals working in harmony to achieve the collective goals of a group, in this case the literacy plan. It's a structure in which individuals, depending on their talents, skills, and expertise, are counted on for knowledge, expertise, and advice to assist the group in meeting its goals. It is based on actions intended for the collective growth and doesn't involve a hierarchy of power. In the interactions, no one gives up autonomy or power and there is a mutual respect for contributions of the individuals.

To further illustrate the meaning of shared leadership, Figure 7.1 explains the paradigm shift in leadership, comparing classical or traditional leadership to shared leadership. Although it will take some time for the shift to be universally imbedded in practice, and staff who do not understand shared leadership might view those the principal turns to for assistance with skepticism, sharing of this chart could help still the waters of mistrust. All staff members, hesitant or not, can see from this comparison that they can all have a place in the leadership of literacy instruction.

USING A TEAM APPROACH

Keep in mind that the team approach is a type of shared leadership. A team of staff members who have a set of skills or knowledge in a particular area can effectively move literacy instruction along. For example, if a teacher or group of teachers is making excellent use of the literacy instructional block, the rest of the staff could benefit from the expertise presented to them at a session. The information could be shared at a regular staff meeting or at a planned professional-development or problem-solving session. The result is an improved understanding of the ways to plan for literacy instruction by the staff and a more efficient allocation of time within that block in each classroom. If a team is presenting, the team members could divide the presentation tasks of the workshop and then individually offer assistance to others in a coaching role. If the school has a culture of sharing, this will occur quite smoothly. If not, presentations by individuals or teams could be viewed with some skepticism, and the staff needs to be prepared. This could mean the principal praising the efforts of all teachers and reinforcing the professional learning community concept. The material on teams covered in Chapter 8 and appreciation for shared leadership as discussed earlier may also help alleviate negative feelings.

System Opportunities

Many jurisdictions have adopted a model in which schools have an identified literacy contact, lead teacher, or coach. This is a teacher who has specific expertise in literacy who can supply support to the school staff. This person, by accepting the role, has agreed to share leadership. Depending on the structure of the model, the teacher is often seconded to work and learn with other lead teachers at a central location and then is responsible for taking the professional development back to the school or out to the

Figure 7.2   Role of the Literacy Lead Teacher

The literacy lead teacher does the following:

- Coordinates school staff development for teachers related to the literacy program
- Attends any district staff development for literacy contact teachers and shares knowledge with colleagues
- Provides release time for colleagues during scheduled lead teacher time to permit a colleague to attend district staff development
- Models teaching strategies for teachers in the classrooms
- Schedules, sets agendas for, and chairs in-school literacy meetings
- Liaises with special education support staff to adjust the program to reflect individual student literacy needs
- Works with the principal to use data from literacy assessments (e.g., state/province, district, school) to identify focus areas for literacy
- Provides leadership in the implementation of system and state literacy programs

---

rest of the system. The lead teacher is an invaluable resource to the principal and the school but is unfortunately viewed with some mistrust by other staff members who suspect favoritism or a hidden agenda. The principal can help facilitate an understanding and appreciation for the resource by defining the role of the literacy lead or coach to avoid confusion or unexpected demands. Figure 7.2, after adjusting to match the district's phraseology and model, can help with this task.

In-Service Management

School districts often offer extensive, voluntary, after-school literacy training. Conscientious staff members often feel the pressure to attend the majority of the training. This is often a self-imposed, unrealistic expectation but speaks well of their desire to be the best literacy instructors. There are also principals who, wanting to be well informed to help the literacy plan move ahead, try to attend every event with their staff members.

The first step of a successful strategy to help relieve the pressure to attend every session is for the staff to collectively look at the staff development calendar for the district and divide the responsibility to attend the training sessions. In this way, at least someone from the school is in attendance at the session. To address unexpected opportunities not on the calendar, a system of taking turns from a list could be used. This does not preclude an individual teacher from attending as many workshops as desired but does ensure school representation at each training session.

The second step is that after returning from the training, the teacher responsible for attending puts his or her name on the front of the handout materials and make copies for the staff members who didn't attend, including the principal if necessary. A binder, supplied by the principal, is given to each teacher to store the material for easy reference after reading through it. Should a teacher have any questions or need clarification, the teacher who signed the front page is now the local "expert" who can help. Depending on the topic and nature of the material, some strategies can be implemented without further input; others may require the attending teacher to share information at a staff meeting. The development of individual literacy binders relieves the anxiety to attend all of the training and puts into each teacher's possession a valuable and informative resource.

TEACHERS LEARNING FROM TEACHERS

It is widely accepted in adult learning models that adults learn best when information is relevant, useful, and from a peer. By putting a structure in place for sharing, even the most reluctant of staffs can become active learning communities.

The roundtable discussion group described in Figure 7.3 is designed to facilitate sharing of successful literacy instructional strategies and has successfully been used in a senior school to reinforce the principle that literacy is every teacher's responsibility regardless of grade or subject area. The session is invitational and whether initiated by the principal or not, principal attendance is strongly recommended to keep up with what is happening in the classrooms.

After beginning the sessions, nonattending staff will begin to see the useful ideas and teacher-ready materials and hear from the participants of the positive, nonthreatening atmosphere. They may also hear from the students about the excitement of using the beneficial methods in classes of the participating teachers. Some

Figure 7.3   Roundtable Discussion Group on Teaching and Learning

Goal

To share teaching and learning strategies in an encouraging, supportive, and nonthreatening environment

How it works

The staff is invited to attend an informal roundtable session where colleagues share, explain, or demonstrate a learning/teaching strategy that others may not have seen or used before. The strategy may be general or specific and may deal with literacy instruction topics such as strategies, resources, grouping, concept development, or warming up a lesson, or may focus on a specific theme identified for that session. Presenters share their ideas in fifteen minutes or less and provide a handout that addresses the following questions:

a) What is it?
b) How does it work?
c) How can it be applied?

Criteria—The strategy should

a) Have application to literacy across the curriculum
b) Engage students
c) Promote higher-order thinking
d) Be designed to ensure that all students can experience some degree of success
e) Have meaning for all students

To promote the success of the discussion group, the facilitator should keep the following suggestions in mind:

- Ensure that the sessions last no more than one hour in length and that timelines are adhered to.
- Find a comfortable location such as a library or seminar room. Some information is best shared in the classroom where something posted on the wall is integral to the presentation.
- Openly state that the only rule of these sessions is that the comments remain positive, and though suggestions for extension are welcome, the roundtable is intended to celebrate and support colleagues as we learn from them.
- Advertise and thank presenters and participants through newsletters, memos, and a letter for their file.
- Provide a brief handout for each strategy that participants can take away with them. Provide some kind of binder or file folder to store their materials. Keep an organized binder of all the strategies presented because others who missed the session may ask for these resources.

- Make it easy for presenters. Photocopy materials and organize getting VCRs, overheads, or chart paper.
- Provide an evaluation sheet so that you can do a better job of getting what participants want. Ask for suggested topics and always ask if they have any ideas they might be willing to present.
- As with any new strategy, expect things to begin slowly. The first meetings may only draw a few participants but by persevering and maintaining a high level of professionalism at the sessions, word will spread and attendance will increase.

---

students will even apply strategies used in one class to an assignment in another, prompting a teacher to begin to see the value of the sessions. The goal is to involve as many staff members as possible, but it is unrealistic to assume that everyone will attend voluntarily.

Many factors will affect the success of the roundtable sessions. The size of the staff, individual personalities, and the openness to each other will have an impact. The timing for initiating the strategy could be in conflict with many other initiatives that are presently demanding teacher time. If initiated by the principal, the sessions must be seen as authentic and not for ulterior motives such as teacher performance appraisal. A school that has a culture of sharing or an active professional learning community will have far less difficulty beginning sessions such as the roundtable. An additional benefit of the sessions is the opportunity for future leaders to emerge. Teachers, given the opportunity to act as instructional leaders, may discover that curriculum or administrative leadership is a goal they wish to pursue.

SUMMARY

A principal, using the right strategies, can easily share leadership in literacy. By drawing on the expertise of others, the principal does not have to be the expert in all areas. By participating in the sessions run by staff members, the principal also grows professionally and understands the curriculum content and effective strategies of literacy instruction. Teachers gain confidence and self-worth through shared leadership, inspiring them to seek further professional development. The result of shared leadership is establishment of a culture of professionalism in which the teachers take ownership and responsibility for their own professional growth and student achievement in literacy. In such an environment, professional learning communities thrive and literacy instruction improves.

These teams of teachers, working together as a professional learning community, are addressed in the next chapter. There are tools that can be used to help teams of teachers work productively in a focused manner rather than leaving growth to chance. These tools and guidelines for teams are presented for consideration.

CHAPTER 8

Building Effective Teams

Coming together is a beginning. Keeping together is progress. Working together is success.

—Henry Ford, inventor and industrialist

L iteracy leadership is not only shared with individuals but also with groups or teams of staff members. Increasingly, schools have been working at becoming professional learning communities: a format that facilitates staff engaging in continuing professional dialogue, sharing of expertise and materials, and honing teaching skills. Students in these schools benefit from the ongoing professional interaction as it encourages and fosters the collective growth of teachers as they discuss, practice, and evaluate teaching strategies that result in improved student success.

For a truly vibrant learning community, structures must be in place to promote the interaction of teachers. The work of Robert Eaker and Richard and Rebecca DuFour (e.g., DuFour, DuFour, Eaker, & Karhanek, 2004; Eaker, DuFour, & DuFour, 2002) has been an inspirational source of strategies to help school administrators create and sustain learning communities. This chapter will guide you through the creation of effective teams, principles for them to function by, and tools to determine what is needed to help them meet with success. As the instructional leader in the school, encouraging, promoting, and helping these teams will help you accomplish your responsibilities and spell success for the literacy plan.

Teaching can be a very isolating experience. Teachers usually work alone in their classrooms for most of the day with their students. After school, many work on their own planning for what and how to deliver curriculum the next day. In a small school with only one class per grade, the teacher is even more isolated, without a same-grade teacher to share with. In large schools, divisions or departments can also become closed units, having little contact with the other grades or subject areas. There are times when the whole school staff may get together in the staff room for lunch and staff meetings, but in many schools this is a social gathering and staff meeting agendas can often be monopolized by the business of running the school. As a result, the challenge for the principal is how and when to arrange for staff to work together professionally on curricula.

In the spirit of teamwork and a learning community, the solutions should not come solely from the principal but rather from the members themselves. Initially, opportunities may have to be orchestrated by the principal through release time, creative class coverage, ensuring that a professional development component is included on meeting agendas, and other solutions to make the most of the time in the school day. These opportunities are explored in Chapter 10. If the experiences during these times are meaningful and productive and as teachers begin to value each other as professional resources, they will begin to help devise ways to meet together. When this happens, a professional learning community has bloomed and there may be changes in the conversations in the staff room and hallways to include teaching and learning strategies.

CREATING TEAMS

Promoting the creation of teams can offer different challenges at the elementary and senior school levels. Where elementary schools are usually organized by grade, subjects are generally used to organize senior schools. The size of the school and the complement of staff, traditions, culture, and the location will also have an effect. These create unique challenges and solutions; however, the process to establish learning teams is similar.

Teachers need to see the value of the team approach to improve literacy achievement in students. For some, it will be quite natural as they are in the habit of conversing and sharing with fellow staff members. For others, they need some understanding and incentive as examined in Chapter 5 before embracing a practice. A good starting exercise for a team is a discussion of the questions in Figure 8.1. The questions are structured for the team beginning an examination of current planning and literacy delivery practices, then looking at the team approach, and concluding with the team exploring how it could function as a tool for improving literacy instruction. By initiating the activity, the principal can help the staff realize that they have much to offer each other by creating a plan for how the team will work together and by eliminating any feelings of isolation. Depending on the size of the school, the teams could be by grade, division, subject, or any variation thereof. After the activity, it is interesting to have a whole staff discussion about teams based on what the smaller groups decided. The outcome can be an organization of teams that the staff feels would work best for them. This is then followed by a period of experimentation and a regrouping after a few months to look at the progress and make any necessary changes in the structure. It is recommended that the teams report in some fashion to the principal throughout the process so that you can assist with any problems or information they require. In fact, principal attendance at some of the meetings is a good practice.

The success of this tool is limited only by the skill of the principal to initiate and maintain an atmosphere that encourages open participation. The list may be too long for a single session, and the staff may benefit from having some time to think about the questions prior to the discussion, so they may be distributed at an earlier meeting. Since the staff is integrally involved in the process of establishing the teams, they will, hopefully, not view the formation of teams as an add-on task but rather as a valuable tool. As teams begin their work, principal support and encouragement is critical. Teams should be encouraged to seek information from research and professional activities. As their expertise grows, they

Figure 8.1   Establishing a Team Approach: Guiding Questions

Current structure

1. Do you plan for literacy instruction with other teachers or disciplines?
2. What materials do you use for planning and delivery of literacy?
3. Do you feel that you work in isolation?
4. Are there sufficient supports for you in literacy instruction?

Current knowledge

1. Do you feel comfortable with literacy instruction?
2. Do you feel well-versed in the teaching/learning strategies?
3. How do you assess literacy?
4. What assessment tools do you use?

Team approach

1. What do you see as the benefits of working in teams?
2. What do you see as the challenges for a team structure?

Structure of teams

1. In what areas of literacy do you feel a team approach could be beneficial?
2. What is an effective size of a team?
3. How should team members be determined?
4. How many teams can a staff of this size reasonably establish and maintain?
5. How often, when, and where should teams meet?
6. What could help facilitate team meetings?
7. What are the expectations of the team in regard to keeping the rest of the staff in the loop?
8. What is the expected outcome of a team?

Maintaining a team

1. How long should a team be maintained?
2. How might the membership in a team change?
3. What financial support may a team require?

will gain higher levels of understanding and action. When a principal serves on a team, at least on a part-time basis, staff will be encouraged by the display of commitment to literacy. The teams will need deadlines, but they should be reasonable and are most effective when established and agreed on by the members with the principal.

Guiding Principles for Teams

Successful teams work best under a set of guiding principles. The members agree on these as they begin to work together. Once established, the members are expected to honor them. An example of this is a team in a school that has decided that its goal for the next number of meetings is to discuss how students learn to read and write. To keep focused, team members decide not to let the conversation sway off course. They do not discuss calendar, when certain content is to be taught, or consequences of incomplete work. They choose, rather, to focus on the literacy learning process. They realize that calendar and consequences eventually have a place in the discussion but not until they have a shared understanding of literacy instruction strategies. It is agreed that when the conversation swerves to calendar, for example, it is acceptable for a member to stop the conversation and refocus the members on the issue of student learning processes without any repercussions from the team members. As a result of their guiding principles, they are able to have exciting, focused discussions and in turn accomplish more of their goal in a timelier manner.

Presented with the following guiding principles, a team decides early in the process how they will function:

Specific focus (as in the example above)

Nonnegotiable, established meeting dates

Time limits on meetings or discussions

Static or rotating roles (e.g., the chair)

Shared responsibility to research and acquire materials and resources

Be prepared for meetings

Inviting outside support as required

Record keeping (i.e., meeting minutes)

TEAMS NEED A PURPOSE

Learning teams can develop for many reasons and can be either long term or short term. Some of the most exciting and productive teams are those initiated by a group of teachers themselves to achieve a common literacy goal. Individuals may be involved in a number of teams. For example, a fourth-grade teacher would like to know more about strategies that have been used in literacy in the primary division. The teacher initiates the conversation with one or more primary teachers, and the primary team invites the fourth-grade teacher to its meetings to listen to the conversations. The fourth-grade teacher in turn is able to share that information at a junior literacy team meeting and help create continuity in the program.

A team may also form to investigate a particular literacy issue that affects the whole school. The literacy issue could be one brought forward by the principal or originated from the staff. A team, with representation from each of the divisions, could initially investigate the issue for the staff.

For example, the excerpt below from Elaine McEwan (2001) was presented to a team when it began its research into the issue of raising literacy achievement levels in the upper grades. The team of teachers then worked together to review the source, find other support research materials to collate, draw conclusions, and make recommendations to share with the staff. The task was not to come up with the solution but to equip the staff with the tools to make a collective decision. Sharing leadership on this topic with a team, the principal was able to help the staff work toward the accomplishment of a literacy goal without taking an authoritarian position. The staff felt greater ownership and less pressure to accept the recommendations because they came from their peers.

> Raising reading achievement in middle and high schools is a difficult assignment, even for the most effective instructional leaders. Not only do most adolescents read less as they mature, the majority of their teachers are convinced that teaching reading is not in their job description. With the advent of "high stakes" testing, however, raising the reading achievement of middle and high school students has taken on a new urgency. Without the ability to read well, students face the real possibility of failing their exit exams. (p. xi)

COLLABORATIVE TEAM INTERVENTION

Another effective and common use of teamwork is addressing the literacy needs of individual students. Some students have their progress tracked through a series of meetings that serve to identify areas of difficulty, plan interventions, and report on progress. Most school districts have such a process in place. The meeting members will vary according to the situation, but the goal is common: collaborative problem solving by a team. Regardless of the membership, the principal is one member who should always be present. In fact, many school districts mandate the principal as the chair. This should not be viewed as only a managerial task but as one that requires instructional leadership as you work with the team, sharing expertise and support.

Determining how effective a school's team approach is to addressing student difficulties in literacy can have a direct impact on student success. As the team becomes more productive and efficient, the implementation of intervention improves. Some questions to ask when examining the functions of the team are these: How productive are the meetings? Is the team able to address the literacy growth needs of students with difficulties? Is there good follow-up and communication? The rubric in Figure 8.2 can be used to help a principal and staff members determine their effectiveness and visualize how they can improve.

It is suggested that every person who has participated in a team meeting on student progress complete the rubric independently and anonymously by coloring in the statements in each category that best describe their perspective. Some staff members, such as the principal and the learning resource teacher, will have many meetings to reflect on for this exercise. After selecting the level of each category on the rubric independently, the team should compare and discuss the results. Perhaps what seems good to one person may seem to need improvement to another. After reaching some form of consensus on what is needed, plans should be implemented for improvement. Please note that the rubric, with minor wording changes, could be used by any team to assess how well it functions.

Running effective team meetings to determine student literacy needs makes good use of everyone's time, and participants are more confident in making decisions to help a student. The principal's

Figure 8.2 Effective Team Rubric

	Level 1 Awareness	Level 2 Developing	Level 3 Best Practices	Level 4 Exemplary
Membership	No formal team membership	Inconsistent team membership	Consistent core team membership	Additional team members included to support problem solving process
Time	Informal discussion of students only	Team meets occasionally	Regularly scheduled team meetings	Time limited and student specific team meetings
Process: communication	Staff unaware of purpose/process	Limited awareness of purpose/process by staff	Purpose/process understood by staff	Additional professional development provided for staff on purpose/process
Process: roles/ responsibilities	Not clearly defined	Assigned but limited follow-through	Assigned and responsibilities implemented	Exemplary actions and follow-through demonstrated
Procedure: referrals	Lack of referral process	Incomplete/incidental use of referral process	Regular use of referral process	Consistent/complete use of referral process

	Level 1 Awareness	Level 2 Developing	Level 3 Best Practices	Level 4 Exemplary
Procedure: team meeting	Absence of agenda No formal development, documentation, or communication of action plan	Agenda not consistently established Limited development, documentation, and communication of action plan	Agenda established and followed Appropriate development, documentation, and communication of action plan	Efficient problem solving and planning allowed for in agenda Focused collaboration, development, documentation, and communication of action plan
Procedure: storage of information	Information available but not readily available to staff	Information available to staff	Information available and accessible to staff and generally used to meet student needs	Information effectively and consistently used by all staff to meet student needs
Follow-up	Little or no follow-up	Some responsibilities and timelines met	Responsibilities carried out and timelines for action plan implemented	Consistent monitoring of timelines, responsibilities, and implementation of action plan

participation in this process relays a powerful message of concern and support to the staff and the parents. By continually monitoring and refining practices, the staff and the in-school team do make a difference.

SUMMARY

The structures and uses of learning teams are varied and vast. The team may include part or all of the staff. It may focus on a portion of or the whole topic of literacy, collate research, recommend strategies and resources, and be a forum for professional literature discussion. Regardless, it will definitely contribute to the learning community culture of a school. Whatever structure a team takes, it is a powerful catalyst for change as it gives structure and support for a group of teachers to be exposed to the theory of literacy instruction and to try, evaluate, and discuss new methods and strategies. As the team members and the staff as a whole grow professionally and implement effective instruction, literacy achievement levels in students will increase exponentially.

To this point, you have had the opportunity to examine the principal's role in literacy through gaining an understanding of literacy and balanced literacy instruction, meeting the diverse literacy needs of students, learning strategies to help staff develop a literacy plan, sharing in the leadership within the plan, and using teams effectively. A big part of being an instructional leader is to use all this knowledge to support teachers in the classroom, for that is where all the hard work translates into improved student achievement in literacy. The next chapter will present a number of strategies for the principal to use to fulfill that part of the instructional leader role.

CHAPTER 9

Supporting Classroom Instruction

We are what we repeatedly do. Excellence, therefore, is not an act but a habit.

—Aristotle, scientist and philosopher

Effective classroom instruction is the foundation of literacy development, and principals can play a significant role by supporting the professional growth of all of the teachers. The skill of the teacher to motivate and engage students, to choose appropriate teaching and learning strategies and materials, and to use valid assessment tools and data are fundamental to literacy success. In addition to having the skills, teachers need to believe that they do make a dramatic difference for students. In all of this, the principal can be of support.

It is not uncommon for teachers, especially in low socioeconomic areas, to attribute poor growth and achievement in literacy to the home. The principal, as instructional leader, needs to help teachers rise above using the "poor home life" excuse. The following statement can be used by the school principal in

Figure 9.1   Percentage of Children Who Achieve Success With Varying Levels of Home and Classroom Support

	High Home Support	Low Home Support
High Classroom Support	100%	100%
Mixed Classroom Support	100%	25%
Low Classroom Support	60%	0%

SOURCE: Cunningham and Allington (1999, p.2).

conjunction with the summary of Catharine Snow's study in Figure 9.1 (Snow, Barnes, Chandler, Goodman, & Hemphill, 1991) to stimulate discussion in a staff meeting focused on why students perform differently on similar testing tools such as state or provincial tests. "Research and experience tells us that what the teacher does, day in and day out, minute by minute, has the greatest effect on what children learn. For most children who 'beat the odds,' it was the teacher who made the difference" (Cunningham & Allington, 1999, p. 256). The statement, supported by the study, challenges teachers to assess the impact of their instruction on all children and to look for other factors that affect literacy development.

Snow and her colleagues (1991) provide powerful evidence of the importance of classroom teachers in developing literacy. In *Unfulfilled Expectations: Home and School Influences on Literacy*, they report on a naturalistic study of schools serving students from low-income families. The research team visited homes of children and rated the family support available for literacy learning as high, moderate, or low. They also visited the classrooms these children attended and rated the classroom literacy instruction as providing high, moderate, or low support. Then they examined the effects of different classroom and home environments on children's learning. The table in Figure 9.1 summarizes the impact of two or more years of consistently high-support classroom instruction, a mixed pattern of support (high support one year and low support the next), and low support.

The findings reveal the enormous impact that consistently high-quality classroom instruction can provide. Anything less than consistently high-quality classroom instruction had a dramatically negative impact on the achievement of children from homes in which parents did not provide high levels of literacy support.

Presented with this information, staff should discuss the implications of effective instruction. Certainly it should be reinforced that the teachers are a very influential part of student growth and development. Discussion could be augmented with the sharing of success stories, of times when teachers felt they made a difference and why. Testimonials of best practices such as these inspire others, especially less experienced teachers. It not only helps others but, in the telling of the story, the teacher sharing reaffirms his or her love of the profession and effective instruction.

PROFESSIONAL DEVELOPMENT

Professional development opportunities come from a variety of sources. One that every principal can foster is to devote a portion of each staff meeting to professional development that supports the literacy plan. Finding time in the agenda can be difficult with all the other items that need to be covered. There are creative methods of "doing business" in other ways in order to free up meeting time for professional development, such as quick surveys in the staff-room communication book, online dissemination of information, weekly bulletins, and quick one-item meetings to resolve an issue or make a decision, to name a few. For other ideas, talk with fellow principals; there are many possibilities. The professional development that occurs in staff meeting time can be led by the principal, a teacher, a team of teachers, or an invited guest. Keeping the activity to a schedule is generally appreciated and makes future sessions more welcome.

Another enhancement of professional development is the message that principal involvement and interest relays to the teachers. Credibility as an instructional leader is enhanced when you learn along with staff. Here are some of the many benefits:

1. A clear message is sent to the staff. Staff members often view the principal's attendance as an indicator of the initiative's value.

2. Having attended professional development, a principal is better prepared to visit classrooms and observe. Understanding an initiative allows a principal to understand the observation and give constructive feedback to the teacher.

3. Requests from teachers for materials and resources and the setting of budgets to support a school focus are made easier when a principal knows the needs of the literacy initiative.

4. Knowing the goals and the staff, a principal can help facilitate the establishment of teams. Teachers working together on something new can expedite implementation very effectively.

5. Creating a time table for the school to facilitate a literacy program is more effective when a principal understands the need and uses of a literacy block.

6. When school staff members perform a gap analysis, an informed principal understands and can prioritize the changes required.

7. At staffing time, the principal will know what strengths and skills an incoming teacher will require to fit into and contribute to literacy instruction.

8. Informed principals can be part of the ongoing professional dialogue in a school, enhancing and encouraging a professional learning community.

9. In a formal teacher appraisal program, a principal with a clear understanding of the literacy initiative can encourage teachers and make knowledgeable observations and suggestions.

Action Research

Another type of professional development that a principal can encourage and support is action research. Imagine an action research project that comes about when a teacher wants to understand the best teaching/learning strategies to address a component of balanced literacy. When scores in comprehension on the Grade 6 general literacy test were low, a Grade 5 teacher decided to investigate comprehension strategies and focused on effective prereading activities as a means to increase performance scores. She used selections from five past tests and the practice question for the same tests to serve as pre- and posttest items. After administering the pretest, the students were asked to bring textbooks from other subjects to class to use in the exercises. She selected strategies that were designed to access prior knowledge in context, such as brainstorming, prompting, scavenger hunts, predicting, questioning, charts, word walls, glossaries, and rereading. She wrote,

> As time progressed, I tried to use one, or more, of these strategies on a daily basis. Through subjective observation, I noticed an increase in participation in discussions centered on text-based materials. Students who were initially reluctant to offer responses were taking a more active role in the group and class discussions. Their level of comprehension appeared to be better as well. Both written and verbal responses improved in quality and length.
>
> The administration of the posttest showed an overall increase in reading comprehension for the entire class. Also, the improvement in the quality and length of written and verbal responses appeared to indicate an increased understanding of what they had read. Students' marks between the first and second half of the term showed an upward trend for the majority of the class, with most students maintaining, or increasing, their averages in the second half. Any drops in their marks seemed to be related to lack of effort.

She continued to report that the majority of the students felt they had developed a better understanding of how to use a textbook and find information as a result of prereading activities.

This example illustrates a single teacher looking for ways for students to achieve in literacy. The materials and permission to conduct the research are examples of the support of the principal. Although the sample of students was small and the time frame short, there was enough evidence that teaching specific comprehension strategies can make a difference. The next step was for the principal to facilitate the sharing of this action research project with the staff and to encourage others, individually or in teams, to investigate other strategies in a similar way.

Action research can also be effectively used with a whole school and ensures staff ownership of the project and results. A school concerned about tracing students through the primary grades decided to investigate portfolio assessment. One staff member had heard of the strategy at a conference and felt that it was possibly a solution to the staff concern. With the support of the principal, both in spirit and financially, they proceeded. District support staff with expertise in the area of assessment were brought in to help the teachers select the assessment tools that would be recorded. Time to visit a site in another school district using portfolios was arranged. Materials were purchased so that teachers could determine reading levels, and planning time was created. In the course of the year the teachers became knowledgeable about assessment of literacy skills, selected and tried a variety of assessment tools, chose the most effective tools, made instructional decisions based on the results, accommodated for student needs, applied remediation where necessary, and tracked student progress. They were amazed and pleased at the growth in their students as a result of their efforts and shared their findings with their school district. As a result, the whole district has now adopted assessment portfolios not only in the primary grades but also in junior and intermediate grades as well. This is an example of what the initiative of a few dedicated teachers, with the support of their principal, can accomplish with school-based action research.

Teacher Self-Reflection

An effective tool the principal can promote to help determine future professional development needs as well as direct team discussions and initiatives and make decisions about the purchasing of resource materials is a literacy instruction self-reflection tool based on the district's literacy model. This tool helps a teacher identify areas of personal strength and areas for growth. The following inventory (Figure 9.2) is based on literacy instruction within the four blocks discussed in Chapter 2, Grades 1 through 3, but it could be modified to reflect literacy programs in other divisions (i.e., junior, intermediate, and senior). It may have to be modified to fit the literacy model your school district is employing.

Figure 9.2 Self-Reflection Tool

Grades 1–3 Supported Reading Checklist	1	2	3	4
1 - No implementation, 2 - Partial implementation, 3 - Full implementation, 4 - Ready to share with other teachers				
My focus is on the development of comprehension skills and metacognitive strategies.				
I group students in a variety of ways: small flexible groups, whole group, partners.				
Before Reading: I build/activate prior knowledge.				
I introduce/review key vocabulary (e.g., rivet, word walk, word rate).				
I identify a purpose for reading. (Connects to follow-up activity, see below.)				
I introduce/review and model a "star" strategy.				
During Reading: I encourage students to apply selected strategy(ies) as they read.				
I encourage students to monitor comprehension (e.g., stopping to confirm predictions, to self-question, to clarify understanding).				
When using whole group instruction, I provide support for students who may experience trouble in decoding text (e.g., reading-buddy, choral reading, reader's theater, tutor).				
After Reading: I have students discuss and reflect on use of "star" strategy.				
I provide students with follow-up activities designed to extend and communicate their understanding of text through discussion/graphic organizer/dramatic presentation/written response/other. (See above: purpose for reading)				
I use these techniques/strategies to build comprehension in other subject areas - Social Studies, Science, Math, etc.				

(Continued)

Figure 9.2 (Continued)

Grades 1–3 Teacher Read-Aloud, Self-Selected Reading Checklist	1	2	3	4
My focus is on the development of comprehension, application of metacognitive strategies, and reading enjoyment.				
I read aloud a variety of books with enthusiasm and expression.				
The books I read include a variety of topics and genres.				
The books I read expose students to vocabulary beyond that which they would encounter in their grade level texts.				
I model the use of "star" strategies.				
Students have an opportunity to apply strategies and respond to the text being read aloud.				
The routines for and transitions into independent reading are well-established and effective.*				
Book baskets/tubs include books with a variety of genre, topics, and reading levels.				
Students are reminded to apply strategies to texts they are reading.				
Students read independently or with a buddy/partner.				
All students are engaged in reading.				
Students keep a log of the books they read during this time.				
I read with a small group or conference (may include a reading record) with individual students.				
I keep a record of conference/reading information.				
I conclude the session with a brief student sharing time.				
For Grade 1, independent reading routines and transitions will be developed gradually over the course of the year.				

1 - No implementation, 2 - Partial implementation, 3 - Full implementation, 4 - Ready to share with other teachers

Grades 1–3 Working With Words Checklist

	1	2	3	4
1 - No implementation, 2 - Partial implementation, 3 - Full implementation, 4 - Ready to share with other teachers				
My focus is on the development of skill and metacognitive strategies in the use of the alphabetic principle.				
Grade 1 - I engage my students in a variety of oral activities to develop phonological awareness (rhyming, alliteration games, songs, etc.).				
I address about 4 - 5 letter/sound connections each week. (See **Jolly Handbook** for order.) Sounds are taught and then revisited through word games and writing activities to develop consolidation.* For example: • Students participate in **blending** games and activities, e.g., /s/ /a/ /t/ makes sat, and segmenting activities, e.g., Say the word "sat." What sounds make up the word sat? /s/ /a/ /t/ (See Windows binder for activities.) • Students engage in the multi-sensory blending activity, "word mime." (See Windows binder for details.)				
Grades 1, 2, and 3 - I use the Word Wall daily.				
I introduce 5 high frequency words per week. Steps are as follows: see the word, say the word, chant the word (clap, snap, chant), write and check, trace around word.				
To consolidate automatic recognition and spelling of the Word Wall words, I regularly use activities like **Be a Mind Reader, Wordo,** and others. (See Classrooms That Work and/or Windows binder.)				
I regularly use activities such as **Making Words, Sorting Words, Guess the Covered Word, Rounding up the Rhymes** to promote skill with spelling patterns. (See Classrooms That Work and/or Windows binder for description.)				
*Synthetic phonics (Windows recommends Jolly Phonics) should be used most extensively in Kindergarten (JK/SK) and Grade One. By the time students reach Grade Two, sound/symbol connections should be firmly in place. If there are students for whom this is not the case, additional support must be provided.				

(Continued)

Figure 9.2 (Continued)

Grades 1–3 Supported Writing Checklist	1	2	3	4
1 - No implementation, 2 - Partial implementation, 3- Full implementation, 4 - Ready to share with other teachers				
My focus is on the development of skill and the use of metacognitive strategies in written communication.				
I model writing at the overhead, or on chart paper, • identifying the purpose of writing • drawing attention to use of classroom resources (Word Wall, 6 Traits Posters, etc.) • introducing/reviewing a specific writing skill or form of writing • using the class Editor's Checklist at the completion for brief editing				
I provide instruction and support in understanding and implementing the 6 Traits of Writing. (See Windows binder.)				
I use various texts and trade books to provide models of the effective use of **ideas, voice, sentence fluency, word choice, organization, and use of conventions** (6 Traits).				
I use various texts and trade books to provide models of the different forms and purposes of writing (e.g., letters, narratives, persuasive writing).				
I provide instruction and support in the use of the writing process, including the use of **graphic organizers for planning.**				
In addition to modeled writing, I provide opportunities for interactive, shared, and independent writing.				
I conference with individual students to discuss aspects of their writing.				
At the end of class, some students share their writing - I encourage good speaking skills at this time.				
I model and encourage students to ask thoughtful questions of the author.				
Students have an opportunity to assess the writing of peers and to self-assess their own writing.				
Class and student publications are displayed in the classroom.				

SOURCE: District School Board of Niagara.

The tool is quite extensive. An effective strategy is to have staff reflect and complete the checklist independently, then collectively discuss and make plans from each of the four sections at different times. The whole tool could be strictly for personal use and planning, but in the spirit of professional learning communities, the results could lead to team planning in a specific area of literacy instruction. It may be discovered that one area is already well developed while another needs extensive attention.

It is important to note that the goal of this activity is for individuals to determine the professional development needs and materials required of themselves and perhaps the staff, not for performance appraisal purposes. Individual responses are strictly confidential to the teacher and help the teacher filter and process discussions. The results can also be used as the teacher establishes personal–professional growth goals, helping identify areas for improvement. If staff members wish to discuss their own results with each other and in turn share expertise and/or resources, that should be their personal choice.

Resources Are Not Enough

Integral to the initiation and maintenance of a literacy program is the responsibility of the principal to ensure that adequate resources and the professional development required to put those materials to best use are made available. Print material, kits, and support documents are needed to support the adopted literacy instruction approach. However, even though teachers need good resources, an effective instructional leader does not just make sure enough materials are available. When Dr. Dale Willows of the Ontario Institute for Studies in Education (OISE) recounted visiting some schools in Australia that had been identified as needy in literacy instruction, she was amazed to see the amount of resources that had been supplied. However, perhaps overwhelmed by the volume of resources and not supplied the professional developments to understand and make use of the material, the teachers were, unfortunately, continuing on as usual, and the resources sat unused. Little had changed in literacy instruction, and consequently, the student literacy levels had not improved (personal communication, May, 2002).

It would not be surprising to find that many schools throughout North America also have a wealth of untapped resources supplied by school districts or purchased with the intent to use. Many teachers, however, for reasons such as time constraints, lack of background knowledge, level of self-motivation, and desire to cling to the comfort zone of traditional methods, do not independently use new materials. Even in a school with literacy at the core of their beliefs, professional development is required to stimulate and promote the adoption and use of new resources. The professional development, depending on the material, can take many forms, from a presentation at a staff meeting to a scheduled in-depth workshop. Whatever the format, time and, usually, money are required. An effective instructional leader budgets for materials and teacher in-service training for the use of those materials. It has been said that for every dollar spent on new resources, less than half should be for the materials and the rest should be for training.

When planning the best in-service model to meet the needs of the teachers and move forward in literacy, remember that the greatest impact occurs when participants are given support to follow up on the training provided. Presentation of a theory or information and modeling will only become imbedded in practice when teachers are given the time to implement the strategies and use the materials. Teaming with peers, sharing of expertise and resources, and follow-up progress discussions can help ensure the implementation of a literacy model of instruction.

WALKING ABOUT THE SCHOOL STRATEGY

It is difficult for a principal to support classroom instruction if there is not an understanding of what is happening in the classrooms. Unless a principal has a background in literacy instruction or has been able to attend many in-service sessions, there is likely a need to become familiar with current philosophies and practices. The acquisition of knowledge cannot be left to reading, professional development, informal conversation with staff, and cursory observation in the classrooms. Just as the teachers truly comprehend instruction by doing it, principals need to see literacy instruction in action.

To this end, there is a process of observing a classroom that will result in an increased understanding for the principal with a bonus opportunity for professional growth for the teacher. The process some principals are using is a walking about the school strategy based on the Downey and Frase model (2003). The strategy is a method for turning a short classroom visit, about ten minutes, into a meaningful learning experience for the principal and the teacher. It helps the administrator focus on particular aspects of literacy instruction, student engagement, and learning. Depending on a principal's knowledge and expertise, some notes are made to record observations in the classroom. Recording on an organizer (see Figures 9.3 and 9.4) helps focus the observation in specific areas. Even if the classroom visit is not during a literacy instructional time, elements of literacy instruction from the organizer can be observed. In the process, from the observations, the principal formulates a reflective question. The reflective question guides the professional dialogue that follows at a convenient time between the principal and the teacher—one in which the principal learns about literacy instruction and the teacher grows by reflecting on the choices and decisions that were made for the activity that was observed. The conversation could result in the sharing of strategies with other teachers and planning for future developments.

A critical step before beginning the use of this strategy is to present at a staff meeting an explanation of the procedure, purposes of the walk-about, and the benefits for both the teacher and the principal. It will help dispel anxiety in the staff members by giving them a chance to see how you will record what you observe and that you will give them an opportunity to ask for clarification. It is also a good idea to begin to use the strategy on more open teachers, which gives the reluctant teachers an opportunity to see it in action with positive results. When introducing the process to staff, ensure that you cover the list in Figure 9.5.

To effectively use the walk about the school strategy, principals need practice. Principals in some districts have tried the strategy together, first at one school and then the other, as practice partners for a day. After each brief visit to the classroom, they compare notes and discuss what reflective question could be posed. Ideally, one of the principals has been using the strategy and should have a good grasp of it. This has served to develop confidence in the principals and has led to more effective use of the strategy.

Figure 9.3   Walking About the School Organizer

Walking About the School

Date: _____ Time: _____ Teacher: _____ Grade: _____

Instructional Strategies:
- Direct Instruction
- Modeling
- Strategy Instruction
- Emphasis on Metacognition
- Meaningful Learning Contexts
- Multi-Level
- Multi-Sensory
- Discussion—large group
- Discussion—small group
- Other: _____

Curriculum Expectation(s):

Student Engagement:
- Working independently
- Listening
- Questioning/answering
- Discussing
- Group work
- Activities
- Other: _____

Wall Walk - Supportive Environment:

Notes:

I wonder:

Model for Literacy Instruction
- Working With Words
- Supported Reading
- Supported Writing
- Teacher Read and Self-Selected Reading

Bloom's Taxonomy of Cognitive Skills
- Evaluation
- Synthesis
- Analysis
- Application
- Comprehension (lowest level of understanding)
- Knowledge (memory)

SOURCE: District School Board of Niagara.

NOTE: Refer to Figure 9.4 – Guide to Using the Walking About the School Organizer for clarification of the sections of the form and their intent. This will help you use the tool effectively.

Figure 9.4 Using the Walking About the School Organizer

The following notes will help you make use of the form in Figure 9.3.

1. Instructional Strategy Box

You may see one of the following strategies being used. Over a number of visits you would hope to see a variety of them. You may choose to ask for more information about the strategy from the teacher (i.e., why it was chosen, why it is effective, how it enhances literacy learning).

Instructional Strategy	Looks Like
Direct instruction • What and why	The teacher identifies and explains the purpose, steps, and characteristics of the learning task.
Modeling • How—make thinking and problem solving visible	The teacher demonstrates how a task is to be completed and "thinks aloud."
Strategy instruction • Opportunities to learn about, observe, practice, reflect on, and discuss use of strategies	The teacher introduces, models, provides opportunities to practice, and reflects on the use of the strategy.
Emphasis on metacognition • Opportunities to practice the skill orally and in writing	The teacher models metacognitive behaviors (think-alouds, written reflection) and supports students with opportunities to share their thinking.
Meaningful learning contexts • Including reading and writing tasks that motivate and allow students to apply their skills	The teacher provides authentic learning experiences and choices in reading and writing that allow for application of skills.
Instruction that is • Engaging • Intellectually stimulating	Instruction/activities engage students' attention and interest.
Multi-level • Helps address a range of levels	Instruction/activities support and allow for varying levels of skill/understanding.

(Continued)

Figure 9.4 (Continued)

Instructional Strategy	Looks Like
Multi-sensory • Motivates, engages, and supports memory	Instruction/activities support auditory, visual, tactile, and kinesthetic learning.
Use of discussion • Clarifies, enhances, and extends understanding	The teacher facilitates and supports discussion as necessary among large and small groups and partners.
Scaffolding • Enables students to achieve success that would otherwise be out of reach	Students are provided with appropriate support to achieve success.

2. Wall Walk—Supportive Environment

Observing the materials on the walls of the classroom (e.g., student work, word wall, anchor charts) is a way to gain more knowledge of curriculum expectations and learning strategies. The principal may be curious about a particular item and could ask for information about the value and uses in the "I wonder" discussion.

3. Curriculum Expectations

Observer identifies the curriculum expectation. If unsure, this would be a point of discussion from which the principal could learn more about the curriculum.

4. Student Engagement Box

This is not an observation of *if* they are engaged but rather of *how* they are engaged. Keeping a record of whether or not students are engaged, and to what degree, is evaluative in nature and is not the purpose of the observation. Over a number of visits it is hoped that the students are observed engaging in literacy learning in a number of different ways. An "I wonder" question could come from the curiosity of the principal about a particular type of activity and its merits and uses.

5. Notes

All aspects of the organizer may not be observable each time a class is visited. The organizer only serves to help the observer focus and reminds the observer of some of the potential things that may be seen. It is important to note that the information recorded and the question posed should not be evaluative in nature. The discussion with the teacher should be of a tone that invites discussion and will lead to further conversation. Not all teachers will be comfortable with the format as they may not be used to talking with the principal about classroom instruction in any other format other than in the teacher-performance-appraisal process. It is best to start with more open teachers. As they share with their colleagues about the value and nature of the conversations, more reluctant teachers will follow suit. Hopefully, the conversations the principal begins with this process will be extended to teachers sharing with each other in the spirit of a professional learning community.

6. I Wonder . . .

After a visit, a reflective or "I wonder" question should be phrased so that it asks about an observed teaching choice and the teacher's reason for choosing it. For example, "Please tell me about the strategy that you were using when the children were practicing the word-wall words. Why do you use this strategy and how effective do you find it?" focuses on a particular strategy that the principal would like to learn about and directs the teacher to consider the choice of the strategy. The question does not include "I liked . . ." or "I am concerned about . . ." phrases that are evaluative in nature.

7. Model for Literacy Instruction and Bloom's Taxonomy Boxes

These boxes are for reference and reminders of the components of the literacy program as well as reminders that teachers are encouraged to engage students in activities and talk that requires high levels of thinking.

Regardless of the observation model chosen, a primary goal is for the principal to gain a deeper understanding of literacy instruction. The nature of the exercise makes the principal visible in the school and broadcasts an interest in curricula. Conversations with teachers enhance their comfort level, reinforce their importance to the learning process, and model professional learning communities. Knowledge gained will increase the ability of principals to make viable decisions on how to best support classroom instruction.

Staff Supervision

Each school district has some sort of teacher appraisal program. It may be unique to a school or comply with a district-mandated model. Regardless of the format, teachers should be encouraged to include some aspects of the literacy plan into their personal goals. As literacy is likely on a district's strategic plan and subsequently on a school's improvement plan, it only follows that the teacher should see literacy as a personal professional goal. By selecting a literacy professional goal, the teacher will likely have

Figure 9.5   Introducing the Walking About the School Strategy
to Staff

---

1. **Rationale**
   - Need for administrators to be aware of and understand literacy curriculum and teaching strategies
   - A structure to encourage professional reflection and dialogue with teachers

2. **Choice of strategy**
   - Tool that is time manageable, unobtrusive, meaningful, and nonjudgmental

3. **What it is**
   - An opportunity to learn and grow together
   - An enhancement of curriculum delivery
   - A positive experience

4. **What it is not**
   - An opportunity to "fix a problem" (if needed, that occurs in a different structure: the teacher-appraisal program)

5. **Process**
   - Short five- to ten-minute visits
   - Quick notes taken (share organizer or method to be used)
   - Follow-up reflective question
   - Ongoing dialogue

6. **Questions of clarification**
   - Opportunity for staff to ask questions about the process

---

many opportunities for professional growth and support through a district in-service program. Once personal goals are established, principals have a duty to see the performance appraisal through to completion. This is a particularly useful way for a principal to encourage a teacher who has been reluctant to embrace the literacy initiative to participate.

Whether a teacher is on a formal performance-appraisal program or not (in some districts there is a cycle), the principal is responsible to supervise staff as required by regulation. Supervision should be viewed as a positive experience and an opportunity for growth. The skill of the principal to develop and foster this type of relationship will impact the culture and climate of the school and subsequently affect literacy instruction.

SUMMARY

Many strategies for instructional leadership in literacy have been presented, including individual and team approaches. The ideas presented are to serve as springboards for you to use in the areas that you feel would be most beneficial to you and your staff. They are designed to help you establish credibility in the school as an instructional leader, not just as a school manager.

The final chapter addresses one of the most common excuses used for not implementing change: time constraints. Despite the principal's best efforts to initiate change and encourage staff, it often comes down to discovering ways to find the time to accomplish the goals set out in the literacy plan. Even though the implementation of learning strategies plays out during regular instructional time, the time required for professional development and for teams to meet, discuss, learn new strategies, and work together must be addressed. Chapter 10 will give you ideas to help you creatively solve this problem.

CHAPTER 10

Resolving Time Issues

We must use time as a tool, not as a crutch.

—John Fitzgerald Kennedy, statesman

It is not uncommon to hear teachers say that, considering the size of curriculum they have to cover, the marking they have to do, the reporting that is required, and the preparation needed, there just isn't enough time to meet as a team. The challenge of planning for and delivering all the subject areas and giving each its due has often been a major barrier to the implementation of school initiatives. To eliminate this barrier, effective literacy instruction needs to be viewed as a means to the end. Literacy skills can be taught and applied in all parts of the curriculum as they enhance and increase a student's ability to learn. Students with good literacy skills can more easily and rapidly advance through the curriculum independently, selecting strategies that accomplish tasks and requiring less teacher assistance. In short, working at improving literacy skills will enhance learning in all subject areas. If this is part of the belief system of the school, teachers are more likely to feel that time spent in professional development on literacy is an investment in student success.

Even when teachers have embraced an initiative, it is still important that the principal takes measures to create a timetable that optimizes both instructional and planning time. Carving out time during the day for staff to meet and have professional dialogue is a challenge; however, adjusting how time can be spent through creative time-tabling and making room for teamwork sends a powerful message to the staff that the principal values growth in literacy instructional practices. The suggestions that follow have all been successfully implemented. They were developed out of need and comply with mandated instructional time of the school districts. Each required rethinking of the structure of the day.

GIVE UP SOME TIME, YOU GET SOME TIME

In one senior school, the teachers and administration came up with a compromise. After agreeing that setting a time each week for teachers to work together was very important, the teachers, with the principal's support and permission, decided they could create a planning period of forty minutes once a week that would begin to meet twenty minutes before the morning bell and continue through the first twenty minutes of the instructional day. During the twenty minutes of the instructional day that students were now without teachers, the principal, vice principals, and guidance and special education staff took all of the Grade 9 and 10 students for a program developed to help students establish and achieve academic goals, while the Grade 11 and 12 students had a study period. A compelling case was made, and the district and parents approved the plan. All the parties agreed that the time spent by the teams of teachers directly translated into more effective teaching and increased literacy skills in the students. It also satisfied the requirements for a program on goal setting and the development of independent study habits. As with any plan, progress was monitored to ensure that student success was not being compromised. The teams met on schedule and self-regulated the focused discussion. As mentioned earlier, this required the team to set guidelines for valuable professional growth. The increased skills of the teachers, the cohesiveness of the program, and the shared responsibility for literacy are all testaments to the plan's success.

Unfortunately, a plan as described above left the principal and vice principals out of the discussions. It also excluded the learning resource teachers and the guidance teachers who were used in the advisory program and to supervise study hall. A similar exclusion of staff can be found in an elementary school that has the music teacher work once a week with all the students of a division in a choir in order to release the teachers for a team meeting. There are also schools in which principals supervise large groups of students in buddy reading programs to release teachers. In all these cases, it was agreed that the value of teams meeting during the school day outweighed the exclusion of the individuals. It was also established that the student activities addressed some portion of the curriculum. For school cohesiveness, there was a process developed by which the excluded individuals were able to keep informed about the discussion and decisions of the teams.

THE BALANCED SCHOOL DAY

Another school, this time elementary, is an excellent example of a staff and principal completely thinking out of the box and implementing a timetable that addressed a number of issues. To address these concerns, primarily establishing a daily literacy block, they investigated block scheduling. What they dubbed "the balanced school day" was implemented, modified, and adopted. It is now a model that many schools are using.

The staff and principal of the school identified a number of areas of concern. They wanted to make the best use of the instructional day, and they were concerned about the decreased energy level of the students in the last portion of the day and how that affected learning. They wanted to increase the physical activity of the students and promote better nutritional habits. They also wanted to create large blocks of uninterrupted time for literacy instruction. Finally, the time wasted each day in transitions was worrisome. While maintaining a mandate of three hundred instructional minutes each day, ninety minutes for lunch and recesses, and the teacher-collective agreement for a forty- minute uninterrupted lunch break for each teacher, they planned to restructure the entire day. The resulting timetable in Figure 10.1 illustrates how they were able to meet all the requirements while taking a somewhat untraditional approach to time-tabling.

Figure 10.1   The Balanced School Day

Time	Activity	Instruction Time	Break Time
8:45–8:50	Announcements		
8:50–9:40	Period 1	50 minutes	
9:40–10:30	Period 2	50 minutes	
10:30–10:50	Nutrition break		20 minutes
10:50–11:15	Fitness break		25 minutes
11:15–12:05	Period 3	50 minutes	
12:05–12:55	Period 4	50 minutes	
12:55–1:15	Nutrition break		20 minutes
1:15–1:40	Fitness break		25 minutes
1:40–2:30	Period 5	50 minutes	
2:30–3:20	Period 6	50 minutes	
3:20	Dismissal		
		Total 300 min.	Total 90 min.

NOTE: The timetable starts and ends at a traditional time. This is important if the school shares a bussing schedule with other schools.

The biggest difference between this and a traditional timetable is that instead of two fifteen-minute recesses and a lunch period of sixty minutes, there are two forty-five-minute fitness/nutrition breaks. The students are required to bring lunches that will span both nutrition breaks. This should not be more food than traditionally brought to school to cover two recesses and a lunch but the same amount, packed differently. It has been found that at each break, the students eat a more balanced minimeal rather than a nutritional lunch and two, often sugary, recess snacks. The local health units provided publications to help parents know what to pack. If a student was able to go home for lunch, one of the breaks was designated for that purpose. Parents and the crossing guards were made aware of the times. As a bonus, it was discovered that the schedule also allowed time for an enhanced intramural sports program in the school. Rather than all divisions vying for time at the midday period, there are now two periods each day when the gym can be used. By spreading nutrition and physical activity out during the day, it has been found that students are as astute and able to learn as effectively in the last part of the day as at the beginning of the day.

The three back-to-back fifty-minute instructional periods create three one-hundred-minute blocks. This offers the teachers flexibility to schedule the delivery of curricula as necessary for the class. With the scheduling of the gym, library, and computer lab throughout the day, each teacher was able to maintain a daily one-hundred-minute literacy block, and even if it was later in the day, because of the nutrition/fitness breaks, the students were prepared to learn. Even in a school with a substantial amount of rotary-delivered subjects, the fifty-minute periods were preferred because less time was wasted in transition. Teachers and students surveyed favored the extra time in each subject to consolidate information and complete assignments.

An additional bonus to the balanced day is the ability, through the supervision timetable, to free up staff by division for team literacy meetings. For example, on the duty schedule, the teachers on a team were scheduled so that none of them had duty during the nutrition/fitness break on at least one day of the week. This allowed them to have a forty-five-minute literacy-team-planning period as well as a contractual lunch period on that day. The teams of teachers found that they were able to accomplish much more in an uninterrupted period of forty-five minutes than over three fifteen-minute recess breaks. This was also preferred to meetings after school when teachers were tired and felt the need to prepare for the next day was more important.

As with any plan of this nature, it is necessary to gain the support of the teachers, the parents, and the school district prior to implementation. Presently, a number of school districts have adopted the structure in all its elementary schools and many others have an increasing number of schools using the timetable. Wherever the balanced school day is being adopted, close monitoring of student achievement is maintained to support the decision. Studies are required to prove educational benefits of the approach, but based on discussions, students and teachers feel more productive and the literacy block is seldom compromised.

Even scheduling in a traditional timetable should strive to accommodate long, uninterrupted literacy instruction blocks and facilitate the meeting of literacy teams. Consider a common preparation period for same-grade or divisional meetings once a week or a cycle made possible through a rotary subject schedule.

Regardless of how meeting time is arranged by the principal, the use of school day time has two benefits. First, it communicates to teachers the importance of teamwork, and second, it gives teachers an opportunity to work together when they are fresh, rather than at the end of an exhausting day. Finally, it is important to repeat that when the teams meet, there needs to be purpose and focus to the discussion. The literacy teams need to seek answers to questions such as these:

What do we want the students to learn?

What are the best strategies/methods for teaching?

What strategies do the students need to use consistently?

How do we know that they have learned?

What will we do when they don't learn?

SUMMARY

A supportive principal willing to work with staff to investigate and consider alternatives to resolve the common issue of time allocation is absolutely necessary. The framework of time needs to work in harmony with the framework of literacy planning and instruction. It is within the principal's control to help make that happen. Through a greater understanding of literacy instruction and of the value of teams of teachers in professional learning communities, many instructional leaders and the staff will begin to appreciate the benefits of using an adjusted timetable to optimize the school's use of time.

Afterword

Are You Up to the Challenge?

Do not wait; the time will never be "just right." Start where you stand and work with whatever tools you may have at your command, and better tools will be found as you go along.

—Napoleon Hill, motivational author

School districts across the continent have risen to the demand to improve literacy achievement for all students. Dedicated educators have studied the results of the research, analyzed data, collaborated on decisions, adapted and tried instructional models, and reflected on the results of their efforts. Regardless of the literacy model adopted, one thing is constant: Students benefit in schools where there is a principal who is an instructional leader and where there is a vibrant community of professionals united by common values, beliefs, and goals. As the teachers, with the encouragement, guidance, and support of the principal, continually seek even better ways to teach, share strategies and expertise, support each other, make data-directed program choices, and learn from doing, students experience a wide variety of research-based learning experiences that build sound literacy skills. Literacy programs in such schools address the needs of individual students, are exciting and motivating, involve parents, and above all, get results. It is hoped that this book has supplied you with some of the tools you can use to lead a school to a high standard of literacy instruction that focuses on developing literacy in all students, preparing them for academic pursuits and life as productive citizens.

Principals need to accept the challenge and be effective instructional leaders, using all of their skill and knowledge to help achieve success for all students and teachers. It is more than a challenge, however; it is, as Michael Fullan (2003) puts it, a "moral purpose" (p. 35).

Must Reads

The content of this book is a result of personal experience with the guidance of information, concepts, and strategies gleaned from many sources, including the following publications. They are highly recommended reading to enhance your understanding of instructional leadership in literacy. The books are arranged alphabetically by title; therefore, the list does not imply any order of importance or sequence for reading. The list is just a starting point as there are many excellent professional books available on the topics covered here. Your selection of books to read will be personal and needs driven.

Breakthrough: Fullan, Hill, and Crevola (2006)

Breakthrough examines a new method for approaching educational reform to help educators create focused instruction, transform classroom experience, and raise and sustain increased performance levels for students and teachers. The book proposes a triple P core breakthrough framework: personalization, precision, and professional learning with an emphasis on data-driven instruction.

Getting Started: Reculturing Schools to Become Professional Learning Communities: Eaker, DuFour, and DuFour (2002)

The authors focus on the cultural shifts that must take place as schools move toward becoming professional learning communities. They offer practical, tried strategies for implementing the change and finding time for the transformation.

Learning Places: Fullan and St. Germain (2006)

This is an easy-to-use guide of practical strategies to promote and create a culture of learning in a school involving the students, teachers, and parents. The strategies are explained and include many ready-to-use materials.

The Literacy Principal: Leading, Supporting and Assessing Reading and Writing Initiatives:
Booth and Roswell (2002)

David Booth and Jennifer Roswell offer administrators the background of effective strategies they need for building more literate students. It shows principals how to evaluate and support literacy initiatives that create more successful learners. The authors profile leaders who have successfully affected their schools' literacy environments.

The Moral Imperative of School Leadership:
Fullan (2003)

The principal is pivotal to change in a school. Michael Fullan examines the traditional role of the principal and suggests that it be recast to one in which the principal plays a more active role within the school and the larger school system.

Schools That Work: Where All Children Read and Write:
Allington and Cunningham (2002)

Drawing on their experiences as teachers, administrators, researchers, and school consultants, Allington and Cunningham provide a framework for the redesign of organizational support toward the goal of ensuring that all children learn to read and write. They describe the critical features of school organization that support or impede the development of effective educational settings.

Seven Steps to Effective Instructional Leadership:
McEwan (2002)

Elaine McEwan outlines seven strategies for a school administrator to use that have a substantial impact on instruction. The practical, hands-on guide helps principals adopt behaviors that research and successful practitioners attribute to successful instructional leadership.

What Great Principals Do Differently:
Whitaker (2003)

Blending school-centered studies with the experience of working with hundreds of administrators, Todd Whitaker describes the fifteen common practices that most successful principals use. He places high value on the interaction between the teachers and the principals as key to successful implementation of change.

Glossary

Balanced literacy is an approach to literacy instruction that ensures that all components of language instruction, technical and aesthetic, are systematically covered with a variety of learning experiences appropriate to the instructional levels of the individuals that include daily reading, writing, word study, and self-selected reading (see Chapters 1, 2, and 8).

Balanced school day is a way to schedule the school day that maintains one-hundred-minute blocks of instruction time, one for literacy, while adjusting the traditional break times to maintain peak performance for students all day. It also accommodates team planning within the school day (see Chapter 10).

Bloom's taxonomy is a model of cognitive skills that assists teachers in questioning and creating assignments that require students to use higher order thinking skills. There are also affective and psychomotor domains that can be considered (see Figures 2.5, 9.3, and 9.4).

Concerns-based adoptive model (CBAM) is a model that can be used to determine the effect that change has on individuals and the implications for the change process (see Chapter 5).

Differentiated instruction is the accommodations that can be used to ensure individual student success by taking learning styles and personal preferences into consideration. These strategies are also considered when differentiating assessment (see Chapters 2 and 3).

Instructional leadership is leadership in matters that are directly related to classroom instruction (see Chapters 1, 4, 5, 8, and 9).

Learning styles are the modes of learning that individuals prefer and can be used to determine differentiation. Generally, the styles are classified as auditory, visual, tactile, and kinesthetic; however, there are many variations and subclassifications (see Chapter 3).

Literacy is defined in a variety of ways, usually including some reference to reading, writing, thinking, and societal contributions (see every chapter).

Literacy lead teacher (literacy coach, literacy resource teacher) is a teacher on staff who has demonstrated extensive expertise in literacy instruction and collaboratively works with the teachers in a school to increase their knowledge and skill in literacy instruction with training through workshops, demonstration, support, and resources (see Chapter 2).

Phonics-based instruction is an approach that emphasizes the mechanics of reading, some claim at the expense of comprehension and appreciation (see Chapter 1).

Professional learning community is a group of individuals who collectively and collaboratively gain knowledge and develop skills in a specific aspect of the profession through a variety of methods (see Chapters 1, 2, 3, 7, and 8).

Reading strategies are methods used by the students in reading to determine meaning and are specifically taught by the teacher (see Chapter 2).

Shared leadership (distributed leadership) is an approach to share leadership among members of a team toward the achievement of a common goal in a positive and hierarchy-free structure (see Chapters 5, 6, and 7).

SMART goals is an acronym for the components of a goal that is specific, measurable, attainable, results-oriented, and time-bound. There are many variations of the acronym that are used to write meaningful goals (see Chapter 5).

Stages of literacy development are the levels of development with precise descriptors that an individual, regardless of age, generally progresses through to master literacy (see Chapter 2).

Whole-language instruction is an approach to language instruction that focuses on language experience that some claim is at the expense of specific learning of the mechanics (see Chapter 1).

References and Suggested Readings

Allington, R., & Cunningham, P. (2002). *Schools that work: Where all children read and write* (2nd ed.). Boston: Allyn & Bacon.

Bernard, J. -L., & Wade-Woolley, L. (2005). *Education for all: The report of the Expert Panel on Literacy and Numeracy Instruction for Students With Special Education Needs, kindergarten to grade 6.* Toronto, Ontario, Canada: Ministry of Education.

Booth, D., & Rowsell, J. (2002). *The literacy principal: Leading, supporting and assessing reading and writing initiatives.* Markham, Ontario, Canada: Pembroke.

Cunningham, P., & Allington, R. (1999). *Classrooms that work: They can all read and write* (2nd ed.). New York: Longman.

Cunningham, P., & Hall, D. (1999). *The four blocks literacy model.* Greensboro, NC: Carson-Dellosa.

Cunningham, P., Hall, D., & Sigmon, C. (1999). *The teacher's guide to the four blocks.* Greensboro, NC: Carson-Dellosa.

Downey, C., & Frase, L. (2003). *Conducting walk-throughs with reflective inquiry to maximize student achievement: Participant's manual.* Johnston, IA: Curriculum Management Systems.

Doyle, M. E., & Smith, M. K. (2001). Shared leadership. *The encyclopedia of informal education.* Retrieved August 5, 2008, from http://www.infed.org/leadership/shared_leadership.htm

Drucker, P. F. (1954). *The practice of management.* New York: Harper.

DuFour, R., DuFour, R., Eaker, R., & Karhanek, G. (2004). *Whatever it takes: How professional learning communities respond when kids don't learn.* Bloomington, IN: National Education Service.

Eaker, R., DuFour, R., & DuFour, R. (2002). *Getting started: Reculturing schools to become professional learning communities.* Bloomington, IN: National Education Service.

Early reading strategy: The report of the expert panel on early reading in Ontario. (2003). Toronto: Ministry of Education. www.edu.gov.on.ca

Fountas, I. C., & Pinnell, G. S. (1999). *Matching books to readers: Using leveled books in guided reading, K–3.* Portsmouth, NH: Heinemann.

Fullan, M. (2001). *Leading in a culture of change.* San Francisco: Jossey-Bass.

Fullan, M. (2003). *The moral imperative of school leadership.* Thousand Oaks, CA: Corwin Press.

Fullan, M., Hill, P., & Crevola, C. (2006). *Breakthrough.* Thousand Oaks, CA: Corwin Press.

Fullan, M., & St. Germain, C. (2006). *Learning places.* Thousand Oaks, CA: Corwin Press.

Hall, G., & Hord, S. (2001). *Implementing change: Patterns, principles and potholes.* Boston: Allyn & Bacon.

Hill, P., & Crevola, C. (1998, January). *Developing and testing a whole-school design approach to improvement in early literacy.* Paper presented at the 11th International Congress for Effectiveness and Improvement, Manchester, UK.

Leithwood, K., Louis, K., Anderson, S., & Wahlstrom, K. (2004). *How leadership influences learning.* New York: Wallace Foundation.

McEwan, E. (2001). *Raising reading achievement in middle and high schools.* Thousand Oaks, CA: Corwin Press.

McEwan, E. (2002). *Seven steps to effective instructional leadership* (2nd ed.). Thousand Oaks, CA: Corwin Press.

Munger, L. (2006). Monitoring change efforts: Concerns-Based Adoption Model (CBAM). In *Administration as a change leader.* Retrieved August 12, 2008, from http://resources.sai-iowa.org/change/cbam.html

National Association of Elementary School Principals. (2001). *Leading learning communities: NAESP standards for what principals should know and be able to do.* Alexandria, VA: Author.

National Institute of Child Health and Human Development. (2000). *Report of the National Reading Panel. Teaching children to read: An evidence-based assessment of the scientific research literature on reading and its implications for reading instruction* (NIH Publication No. 00-4769). Washington, DC: Government Printing Office.

National Reading Panel. (n.d.). *Charge to the NRP.* Washington, DC: National Institute of Child Health and Human Development and Department of Education. Retrieved July 29, 2008, from http://www.nationalreadingpanel.org/NRPAbout/Charge.htm

Nemerowicz, G., & Rosi, E. (1997). *Education for leadership and social responsibility.* London: Falmer Press.

No Child Left Behind Act of 2001, P.L. 107-110 (2001).

Ontario Ministry of Education. (2004). *Literacy for learning: The report of the expert panel on literacy in grades 4 to 6 in Ontario.* Toronto, Ontario, Canada: Author.

Phillips, G. (1993). *Site-based decision-making: Staff and community team-building for continuous school improvement.* Vancouver, BC, Canada: EduServ.

Rogers, E. M. (1995). *Diffusion of innovations* (4th ed.). New York: Free Press.

Snow, C., Barnes, W., Chandler, J., Goodman, I., & Hemphill, C. (1991). *Unfulfilled expectations: Home and school influences on literacy.* Cambridge, MA: Harvard.

Whittaker, T. (2003). *What great principals do differently.* Larchmont, NY: Eye on Education.

Whittaker, T. (2004). *What great teachers do differently.* Larchmont, NY: Eye on Education.

Index

CORWIN
PRESS

The Corwin Press logo—a raven striding across an open book—represents the union of courage and learning. Corwin Press is committed to improving education for all learners by publishing books and other professional development resources for those serving the field of PreK–12 education. By providing practical, hands-on materials, Corwin Press continues to carry out the promise of its motto: **"Helping Educators Do Their Work Better."**

O N T A R I O
P R I N C I P A L S'
C O U N C I L

The Ontario Principals' Council (OPC) is a voluntary professional association for principals and vice-principals in Ontario's public school system. We believe that exemplary leadership results in outstanding schools and improved student achievement. To this end, we foster quality leadership through world-class professional services and supports. As an ISO 9001 registered organization, we are committed to our statement that "quality leadership is our principal product."

DATE DUE